WHY THE F*#@ AM I STILL NOT ORGANIZED?

STOP STRUGGLING WITH CLUTTER ONCE AND FOR ALL

STAR HANSEN

Difference Press

Washington, DC, USA

Copyright © Star Hansen, 2022

All rights reserved. No part of this book may be reproduced in any form without permission in writing from the author. Reviewers may quote brief passages in reviews.

Published 2022

DISCLAIMER

No part of this publication may be reproduced or transmitted in any form or by any means, mechanical or electronic, including photocopying or recording, or by any information storage and retrieval system, or transmitted by email without permission in writing from the author.

Neither the author nor the publisher assumes any responsibility for errors, omissions, or contrary interpretations of the subject matter herein. Any perceived slight of any individual or organization is purely unintentional.

Brand and product names are trademarks or registered trademarks of their respective owners.

Cover design: Carrie Arlah Burr and Star Hansen

Editing: Natasa Smirnov

Author's photos courtesy of Adam Hendershott

CONTENTS

1. Why the F*#@ Am I Still Not Organized?	1
2. Turning Clutter Upside Down	11
3. Taking Your Power Back	23
4. Awaken Your Organizing Genius	33
5. Why Organizing Drains Your Energy	55
6. Managing the Big Feelings That Sideline You Every Time	69
7. Use Clutter to Unblock Every Area of Your Life	93
8. Discover the Message in Your Mess	105
9. Decoding How Clutter Is Actually Helping You	123
10. Stop Struggling with Clutter Once and for All	141
11. The Path Ahead	157
Acknowledgments	163
About the Author	167
Other Offerings by Star Hansen	169
About Difference Press	171
Other Books by Difference Press	173
Thank You	175

For every client who welcomed me into their home. Thank you for all you've taught me and for allowing me to walk beside you. You'll never know the difference you've made in this world, just by being you.

1

WHY THE F*#@ AM I STILL NOT ORGANIZED?

Lina finally shut her computer down after a long twelve-hour day. The unexpected sound of the doorbell paralyzed her. Who could it be? She wasn't expecting anyone. Maybe it's a delivery? No, it's too late for that. Someone at the wrong house? Lina froze and held her breath, hoping they wouldn't hear her and just go away. She scanned the room around her that screamed "no guests allowed." Overstuffed grocery bags crowded the front door. Sprawling stacks of unopened mail lined the hallway floor like grass. She jumped as the doorbell rang again. Someone from outside said, "Lina. Are you there?" Lina closed her eyes, exhaled, and slapped a plastic smile across her face as she wiggled the door open narrowly – as much as the random boxes of who knows what sitting next to it allowed – and popped her head out. It was her neighbor. "Hi, Lina! I made some cookies for you. I was hoping we could sit and have a chat. I hope it's not too late."

Lina felt nauseous. There was no way her neighbor could come in here. It was too mortifying. There was nowhere for her to sit in the clutter-inundated living room.

There was barely room for her right now. Boxes of work files covered every surface, coffee cups from the past few days sat on the TV stand, side tables and even the floor – absent-mindedly placed there from the past few days of work as she hustled to meet a deadline. Exercise gear and kitchen gadgets were scattered everywhere. Her suitcase from last month's trip was still in the middle of the living room with clothes and toiletries overflowing. The state of the house was beyond anything she could let someone see.

Sound familiar? You picked up this book hoping it's the solution you've been looking for. That it contains the missing link for fixing whatever has been stopping you from getting organized. You've done it all – read the books, sparked joy, took entire weekends to purge, binged tv shows, hired an organizer, and cried about it in the shower. But here you are, still pushing the same boxes, bags, and piles around feeling like you're trapped on the crazy-making clutter hamster wheel. You've thought about this a lot, and after all your deep insights, you've decided that maybe it's you. Maybe you're genetically predisposed to be disorganized for life. Sorry, my friend, as smart as you are (and I know you are), that simply isn't true.

You're capable of so much. Look at your work. Look at your family. You've done amazing things in this life. You're positive, loving, kind, and powerful. I know what you're thinking, "You have no idea what a mess I am, I'm way worse than everyone else." Well, let me stop you right there. Please don't compare your insides to someone else's outsides. You have no idea what kind of chaos other people are struggling with, no matter how much they look like they have it all together on social media.

You're a badass in the boardroom (or wherever you're currently shining your light) but would die if anyone ever did a 'drop by' at your house. Clutter and chaos don't match you. It feels like you're living a double life and if people knew the truth about your clutter they would judge, abandon, and shame you. So, you shame yourself before they can. You go on a witch hunt for what's wrong with you. You think if you can figure out what's wrong then you can solve this seemingly unsolvable mystery. And the inner taunts of shame, judgment, and criticism are like cheerleaders, cheering you on trying to get you to cross that finish line. Clutter feels like the worst part of you ... the negative (worst-case) truth of you.

But the real truth is that clutter is the best of you. And if you can start to see what's happening in your clutter your whole life will change.

In twenty or so years of organizing, I've literally never met a disorganized person – and no, you're not the exception. You're just feeling a little lost. The fact that you feel lost right now shows that you're not innately chaotic. If you were, you wouldn't be reading this book. You would be reveling in the magic of living a chaotic life. That would be your dream. The fact that you're uncomfortable in clutter means that you have organization inside of you that wants to come to light. That a deep part of your soul is calling to live another way – and that there is a path that will take you there. Remember, whatever you're seeking is also seeking you. And it won't stop until you come home to that truth. There is a way out of this clutter purgatory. And you deserve better. Look, you may not know the way out of this maze, but I do. And I can walk you through it. You've got your zone of genius, this is mine. Together we will get you out of this chaos – for good.

CHAOS CAN SET YOU FREE

Look, you picked up my book (instead of the bazillion other organizing books out there) because you're ready to see things differently. Something inside of you knows that the way to an organized life isn't found in boxes, drawer organizers, or fancy systems. That there's something *in* your clutter keeping you stuck, and if you can figure it out, then you can set yourself free. I know you want to know what that is. I also know it's terrifying to know that.

Clutter is a powerful cover for much deeper wounds. And your subconscious has tried for years to cover that pain. Touching the clutter band-aid that has been keeping the wounds protected and feeling safe can be terrifying. Especially doing it alone – which is how you've been trying to manage things. It feels too shameful to let people in and let them see the truth, so you do it all by yourself. You put on a smile and make up an excuse for why your book club can't meet at your house this month. You feel mortified when your son brings someone over after school without notice.

But you don't have to do this alone anymore, in fact, it's vital that you don't. But I don't expect you to start celebrating your clutter just yet. I know it's complicated. This is what I'm here for. I want to walk you through your clutter and help you see what I see. Let's discover the solutions that are buried in your clutter.

I'm going to let you in on a secret. Everyone has chaos in their lives. We all just wear it in different ways. I deal with my chaos through my body and food. It's been a lifelong dance with disordered eating and learning to love my body. But that journey is no different than your journey with clutter. The steps are the same, it's just different music. Some people use money, others use relationships, some struggle with technology addiction – if you're human, you've got chaos. And the beauty is that this world was birthed from chaos. If you can wield the power of chaos – to actually use it instead of running from it, you've got a life-changing, transformation tool that will change every area of your life.

Chaos can free you. It can save your life. If you've been struggling with clutter and the fact that you can never seem to make it go away, that means that there's a message in your mess – a special gift. Simply putting things away in well-arranged boxes isn't going to quiet the 10,000 voices screaming at you through your clutter. This struggle is actually a superpower. A gift. It's here because you're meant to elevate in ways you've never expected. And clutter is your path there. You came here to get organized and you're going to leave transformed.

IMAGINE YOUR CLUTTER-FREE WORLD

Imagine a world where your home is organized. It supports you and reflects the best parts of you, your life, and your family. In this magical place, clutter no longer sends you into an overwhelm coma, and when clutter crosses your path, you feel calm and know exactly what to do with it. Imagine a future in which you see and easily solve the things that cause the clutter. Imagine a future where you are impervious to chaos because you've learned how to manage it in a way that only you can. You take those incredible skills that you've used to do great things in other areas of your life, and you apply them to your clutter with ease. You've solved what clutter has been trying to teach you. And you no longer need clutter to get your attention to make big life changes. Imagine being grounded in your power. You no longer have the voices of shame, anxiety, and overwhelm ringing within you anymore. You can hear the calm, strong voice of wisdom within you. Your home is organized, but you're not struggling with its care, management, or chaos anymore. Your home serves and supports you, you don't serve it. You are free to live your life fully, and your home is overflowing with joy, laughter, and life – instead of clutter.

TIME TO SET YOURSELF FREE

The bridge from chaos to calm is not as long and treacherous as you might think. It often feels like a world away. I think this is partly because you've never fully been there before. You didn't experience this as a kid, were never taught how to create it, and you probably haven't known it as an adult. You've experienced it in certain areas of your life and home, but you've never known what it is to live in a true state of clarity and calm. You may have fleeting moments of what it might feel like, but you've never known the lasting experience of it. But you can experience this. And sooner than you would imagine. The beauty is that making peace with your clutter is making peace with yourself. As you do this, peace becomes your common state. The chaos becomes the motivating energy of the moment, the insight that something is ready to change. You no longer wait until the chaos has taken over your life. You can hear the whisper of change and you act on it with ease.

This path is not the one often taken. There are a million books written about getting organized. Some touch on the challenges we face. But few are talking about why we can't seem to get (or stay) organized. And once you know why *you* struggle, you open the doors to set yourself free. Let's have that conversation. The conversation where we leave the superficial world of stuff and enter the deeper conversation of deep and lasting freedom.

IT'S TIME FOR A TRANSFORMATION

The reason you're disorganized isn't what you think it is. And once you see the truth, everything will start to change for you. In this book, we're going to explore the reasons why you're still disorganized, even after all your hard work and many attempts. We'll use that insight to change the clutter narrative and turn that insight into action. As we explore these reasons, I want you to feel seen and understood. I want you to take your power back from the clutter and remember the truth of your power and inherent nature. You're a badass and no amount of clutter could hide or change that.

I know you, even if we've never met. I see you. And I can help you out of this chaos. This book is my love letter to you. To help you remember that chaos and being disorganized isn't a fatal character flaw, that there's nothing wrong with you. This book is here to help you see the real truth beyond the clutter, with the hope that once you see it you can make changes that finally allow you to experience what you've been working so hard for but haven't been able to see yet. This is the turning point in your life. This is the moment where you stop doing what you've always done and instead see things from a new perspective. The perspective that allows you to stop blaming yourself and start experiencing a radical transformation from the inside out.

You deserve a life of joy. No more weekends struggling to get organized after you're burned out from work. No more thinking of excuses to not have people over because you're ashamed of the state of your life and house. No more shoving things into the "room of doom" because someone stopped by unannounced. No more beating yourself up in the quiet moments of your day, seeking out proof of your defects. No. More. It's time to experience the world as it should be. Where you know you're a badass and you use those beautiful skills to provide yourself with the life of your dreams. Where you are not hindered by yesterday's challenges but are free to create what you want when you want.

I wish you could see it through my eyes – the power of all the good things still to come in your life. The best isn't behind you. It's ahead. And the key to that beautiful world is buried in your clutter. I can help you uncover it. I can help you use the clutter to transform your life and set yourself free. I can help you turn a teacup into a new career – a box of paper into the love of your life – a lost letter into emotional peace you never knew was possible. I can help you turn the monster in your closet into a dust bunny that no longer tortures you. I can teach you to see your clutter as the superpower it is and learn how to wield that power in creating freedom in every area of your life. You deserve that. The best is ahead. And everything you're about to learn will shift how you view your clutter, home, and life forever. I know it can be scary to walk this path, to look in the piles and stacks and crevices of your clutter. But I will be with you every step. You're not alone. And I'm not going anywhere. It's not your job to know how to do this. That's my job. I've been doing this for decades and I can lead you through.

Take a deep breath and know that things are about to change. Just by seeing what you're about to see, the chaos will no longer have the same weight and power. And once you shift that perspective, you'll never be the same. Clutter will never be able to torment you again. We'll be working together in tandem to create the life of your dreams. I know that moments will be hard. But you've got this. There's no world where you were born to fail. You are powerful beyond measure. And I will be here, holding the light for you. Your job is to take one step, and then the next. I know the way home and soon you will too. And once you know that path, it can never be taken away again. I've got you. Let's do this!

2

TURNING CLUTTER UPSIDE DOWN

When I was a teenager, my dad's father died. I didn't know him much in life. We lived in another city and family can be ... well, complicated. While the adults were working on the funeral services, I decided to help out by organizing his room. I spent a day decluttering, re-arranging, and making sense of this man I hardly knew. As I went through his piles of paperwork, dresser drawers, and the dish on his nightstand that held his wallet, keys, and watch, I started to see who he was. His books and newspaper clippings showed me he was smart and interested in the world. The broken watches and glasses next to his toolbox, waiting to be fixed, showed me he had a natural aptitude for the mechanics of how things worked. The neat, well-arranged stacks of paper on his desk showed me he was organized and liked to keep things simple. Holding his driver's license, I looked into his eyes and felt like I was meeting him for the first time. I got to know my grandfather after he died by organizing his stuff. I saw who he was, what he valued, and how he lived his life. I was able to know him through his stuff. That was the first time I knew that clutter held insight and wisdom about who we are.

When I was twenty-four I moved to LA to pursue an acting career. I was booking acting jobs but felt like something was missing. I could feel that I had a deep calling that was trying to get my attention. I knew I was a healer, but I didn't know how to express it. I kept asking for guidance and direction to know how to truly live my purpose. One day in acting class, they gave us the assignment to come up with fifty ways to make money, besides working a day job, to drive out the starving artist mentality and any concepts of not being able to make a career from acting. One of the ideas I came up with was a box to organize tax receipts throughout the year so that when you pass off your tax docs to your accountant at the start of tax season, they can easily find your deductions. I only sold one box, but I gained three organizing clients from that idea. I had no idea that there was such a thing as a professional organizer at that time. I just thought, well, I'm good at this. I'm happy to help them out. I loved how it helped people and how easy it felt. Clutter felt like a game to me, and I was able to help bring people relief by doing something that came easily to me. I realized quickly that this was the path for my calling. A place where I could be a healer and help people transform and elevate. Organizing felt like home to me. This is where I discovered that clutter could bring us home to ourselves.

At thirty-one I was thriving as an organizer. I had appeared in over twenty television shows as an expert and was in development for my own TV show with TLC. I had a successful organizing practice in Los Angeles but felt restless. I was so frustrated with people cluttering their lives with organizing solutions. Yes, read that again. It felt like they were simply making their overflowing clutter look pretty – not truly addressing what was causing the clutter. I felt like organizing was actually perpetuating the problem. I felt the call to dive deeper, but I didn't know how. There was a part of me that really loved the attention and validation I received from being a successful organizer and having a presence on TV. My ego was being fed but my soul was still calling for something more.

On a hot day in June, I received the call that would change my life forever. My little sister, Jena, took her own life. I didn't see this coming at all. I knew that she had struggled with mental health challenges, addiction, and suicidal ideation in her life, but I truly thought she was fine right now. We had just talked. She seemed fine. How could I have missed this?

That moment split my life in half. There was the world before Jena died, and the world after. The new world felt like a hole of despair. How had I missed her struggles? How could I have not seen the signs? It took me years to recover. In fact, I'm still recovering and probably will be for the rest of my life. But the death of my sister birthed the most important revelation yet.

When my cousin and I went into her home after she passed, it was like looking at a physical representation of her pain. I could see her struggles in the objects she kept, and those that were missing. Like other suicide attempts in the past, she had gotten rid of almost everything she owned. When we walked in, the house looked almost empty. There were a few items in the kitchen and some basic furniture in the living room. It wasn't until we went into her clothing closet that we found anything personal or emotionally connected to her. Hidden among the clothes were a few photo albums, her favorite books, and some personal gifts given to her from the last year. It was heart-breaking to see my sister's beautiful life reduced to a handful of items. It was like she had erased herself.

Her pain was so strong within herself, but she was able to mask it extremely well to the rest of us. She knew what to say and how to hide her truth. But her house gave her away. It was like looking through the doorway of her pain. This was when I realized that people's struggles reveal themselves through their physical spaces and stuff. That we can see deeper truths in the ways we live and the story of our stuff.

At that moment something came alive in me. I no longer wanted people to suffer in silence. I needed them to know that it was possible to be happy. That they weren't alone. I needed people to feel safe to share their greatest shame and fears, and to know they would be okay – in a way my sister never knew. I needed to know that I was making a difference in people's lives beyond making their homes pretty. At that moment my clutter x-ray vision was born and it's the reason I organize today. I don't care if your home is organized, pretty or fashionable. I care if *you* are okay. What do you need to thrive in your life? The clutter can show us what's needed, and it's my calling to help you see it and help you come home to yourself.

When my sister died, the part of me that needed external ego validation died. The part of me that walked the path of pretty boxes and well-curated systems died. Something deeper was born – a warrior who needs to awaken you from the chaos that has taken over. I don't want you to struggle alone, thinking the chaos is the truth of who you are. It's something you're going through, not who you are. And this path to organization will help you see that and solidify it in you.

You've read the organizing books, watched the shows,

and tried the fads. Let's try something else. Something more true and real.

CHAOS IS CHAOS

Physical clutter has never taken over my life and stopped me from living before, but clutter does pop up from time to time. I look at it and recognize it as I would a friend – a kind loved one that's helping me to slow down, change directions, heal, have fun, find a way through challenging times in a way that aligns with my values – or a hundred other lessons that clutter offers. I learn from my clutter. And I help my clients do the same. I may not experience clutter in the same way you do, but I have my own struggles with chaos. What you feel with clutter is the same thing I feel with my body and my struggles with disordered eating. I know your pain because I feel it too. Mine just looks a little different. I have lived most of my life thinking that if only I could be skinny then my life would be perfect, and I would be happy.

Clutter is trying to teach you something. And if clutter isn't able to get your attention, it will change directions and manifest in another area of your life (body, food, relationships, money, etc.). I know the path you walk, and I can see the way home. That's my calling – to help you use clutter to come home to yourself.

SELF-HELP CAN HURT

I don't know about you, but self-help books, social media, and TV shows often make me feel worse about myself. They leave me with a feeling of inadequacy, and a giant list of things I think I "should" do to get better. I find myself in a state of focusing on what's wrong. I'm going to do my best not to be that to you. I don't want you to stay "hooked" on finding and buying solutions. I want you to shift how you view your clutter so you can free yourself. Remember that TV shows are for entertainment. They have nothing to do with getting organized. I know this from first-hand experience. I've appeared as an expert on over thirty organizing shows. Let me just say that organizing is incredibly boring to watch. The magic of television is in the playing up of the emotional drama and showing pretty, enviable transformations. The story you've been fed keeps you in a shame spiral, thinking that there's something wrong with you. There's nothing wrong with you. Be inspired by shows and the gorgeous before and after pics you see online. Let them awaken your creativity and excitement. But don't think for a second that it's true. You have no idea how many people, how much planning, and hard work go into those thirty-minute shows, glossy pics, and "after" shots. You are one person. Those shows have countless experts, designers, strategists, and a team of skilled workers that contribute to the beautiful transformations you're holding yourself to. See them for what they are, beautiful entertainment meant to inspire and entertain.

CREATING A SAFE SPACE FOR YOU

My job is to go into the areas of your home you don't want anyone to see. The junk drawer in the kitchen, the garage that can't be parked in, the room of doom (the room at the back of the hallway you would be mortified if anyone ever saw). My specialty is whole-home organizing with a focus on women in transition.

I help people transform their homes from shameful caves of chaos into beautiful sanctuaries where lives are built, and parties are held. I help people go through the physical items of their recently deceased loved ones. I help businesses create effective productivity systems. I crawl through spiderweb-filled attics hunting for long-lost family treasures. I help seven-year-olds figure out how to keep their toys organized. I've helped turn cluttered offices into recording studios, overstuffed garages into glamorous gyms, and closets into powerful home offices.

I've seen it all and I don't judge. While digging through people's homes, I've found bags of human teeth, a perfectly preserved dance card from the 1800s complete with suitor signatures, a giant box of butt plugs (I have so many questions there – party favor, single-use, accidental overorder?), dead critters, naked photos of my clients (just try to stay professional after coming across a nude spread eagle photo of your client's husband who is sitting directly across from you), and levels of decomposed foods I hadn't thought possible. I've helped people go shopping for new wardrobes and break open childhood diaries to shred pages containing long-forgotten secrets. I researched what in the heck a miser's bag is, listened to countless stories, and held people's hands as they spent an hour trying to decide if they should keep or toss one single piece of paper. I had to break the news to people that their long-saved beanie baby collection will (in fact) not put their kids through college, and curated countless collections of artwork and unique collectibles. These are some of the things I do from day to day.

But in the face of all of this, no one ever really hires me to organize their home. They may think they do, but they are hiring me to help set them free on a deep level around their stuff. I'm clear with people. I don't organize for you; I organize *with* you. My goal is to fill in the gaps in your organizing education and help see how you might be using clutter to serve some greater need so that you can actually let the clutter go. That's what I'm here to do. I'm part project manager, part counselor, and part manual laborer. And my day is successful when you start to see how clutter may be helping you. That is how I set you free.

The things you think are most shameful would probably not even register on my radar as alarming. My job is to be non-judgmental. I own my humanity like a badge of honor. My own personal challenges are not something to hide, they're "teachable moments." I'll talk about just about anything, and there is nothing you can't share with me. I'm the secret keeper. I know who doesn't think that their husband is the actual father of their child, what you still beat yourself up about from ten years ago, what dress makes you feel like your most authentic self, who was sexually assaulted, and what noise your husband makes that makes you want to suffocate him with a pillow in his sleep. And I take those secrets seriously. That is what I'm here to do – to normalize our humanity and bring some cleansing air to the deep, complex areas within us that we think we need to hide. Because as long as we think we need to hide it, we're going to keep holding onto clutter and chaos to protect us. Air is the single most vital thing we humans need. Without air, we would be dead within minutes. Organizing is like air for our spaces. It creates room for life, vitality, health, and happiness.

I'm a healer. Healing doesn't mean fixing what's broken but remembering your wholeness. And that's what organizing is to me. Helping you remember your wholeness. And clutter has so many clues to do that. I view our work together, not as a task to complete, but as an adventure. We're like Nancy Drew, using clutter to discover clues to solve the mysteries of your life.

Getting organized is a learned skill. I can (and will)

teach you everything you need to know in a short period of time. Clutter is something beyond basic organizing. Clutter stems from something deeper. Clutter offers deep insight that allows you to transform your life. The thing I like about fixing clutter is that it's concrete & practical. Clutter can be changed. When the world feels out of control, it's powerful to know that there's something you can do to see a real, lasting change in your life. And seeing that change occur over and over again, shifts how you think. It expands what you know is possible for you and your life. It changes how you see the world. It gives you your power back.

IS CLUTTER GENETIC?

My mom grew up in a picture-perfect house in the fifties and sixties. My grandfather built their home brick by brick with his twin brother. My grandmother was quite chic and filled the home with beauty and style. My grandma was the quintessential 1950s glam housewife. Her hair, clothes, and home always looked perfect. Even today, my grandma surprises doctors when we go to appointments with her fashionable looks, even at ninety-three. The house followed suit. It's truly a lovely home. But for as lovely as their home was, this was the fifties. Homes weren't meant to be lived in; they were meant to be seen. Rooms weren't meant to be played in, beds weren't allowed to be sat on, and looking good for others was a high priority. As a child in the eighties, I have memories of not being allowed in certain rooms at my grandparent's house or being inspected to make sure we were clean enough to sit down at the table. Despite the rules and museum-like feeling, I loved the picturesque look of my grandparents' house.

When setting up her own home, my mom chose joy over order, and creativity over focusing on what others might think. My parents' house is creative, free, and whimsical. It feels like you're in a fairy wonderland. Each wall is painted a different color, there are photos everywhere, and we were always free to play. My mom is the type of person who will paint a mural on the wall with one of our cousin's kids because she loves creative expression. Both my parents are artists – my mom quilts and paints, while my father creates upcycled welded artwork. In fact, we all have some sort of creative endeavor in my family. I come from a family of artists – everyone had their gift. It wasn't a strange thing to see projects in process sprinkled around the house. Quilts tacked up on the wall, murals sketched out on bedroom walls, mosaic tiles piled in bins according to color, paints out on the counter.

My dad is organized in his jam-packed shop. Mom has order in her chaos. Her office looks like piles of paper, and yet she can find anything she needs, and she has a system for everything. At my parents' house, there is always clutter on the counter – I think it's Mom's comfort zone. My mom needed to create a space where she was free to play. To take her power back from having to live in a museum when she was a child. She has created a world where it's safe to paint on windows, hang ribbons from trees, and tear down walls (literally).

I often call my parents to get their take on systems (tools, hobbies, email, office) because even though it doesn't necessarily look like it, they always have a system. Everyone does. Sometimes we just don't acknowledge it as such. As I've said before I've never met a disorganized person. Usually, people just abandon their systems early because they don't look how they "should." And yet, there is magic in the systems that don't look like systems.

Because I grew up in this type of fun and chaotic environment, I am never phased by clutter. Living in a world where chaos was seen as creative, I never found judgment in clutter. Instead, I see the beauty of someone's life. I can see through the chaos and into the life and creativity there. I can see you in your chaos. Your chaos doesn't feel heavy to me. It feels like a beautiful expression of you. And as much as I can read the story in your clutter, I don't do it unless you ask me to. It's like a switch I can turn on and off. In fact, I can totally go without seeing certain items if I don't think they're mine. I remember my parents bought me a TV for my bedroom in high school for Christmas. It sat in its box, in the living room, unwrapped for three weeks and I never even noticed it. My inability to see the TV was the big joke on Christmas morning.

I share all this to say that I get you. I know how to help you use your clutter to come home to yourself. I want to create a safe space for you to be perfectly imperfect in your journey with clutter. I know what it takes to live a clutter-free life. I'll share what I know, but you know what's best for you. I celebrate you creating a path that works for you. I will share my insights, but it's up to you to take what you like and leave the rest. I'm bringing the ingredients; you're making the cake of your choosing. Trust your gut. I'm here for you. A light home to yourself. You're not alone and we'll find our way together.

3

TAKING YOUR POWER BACK

"If you want different results, do not do the same things."

— ALBERT EINSTEIN

To get you different results, we're going to explore the true reasons why you haven't been able to get organized yet. And the great news is that it will take a lot of pressure off of you and give you a new path to forge. A unique path. If you want different results, you need to try a new path forward. There's a message in your mess and you're about to discover what it is.

I'm here to help bring to light the gut instinct you've been feeling for a while now. That there's something buried in your clutter beyond last month's electric bill and the hand weights you forgot you bought last year. The missing link to getting organized is actually in your clutter. And I'm going to guide you through discovering what's keeping you trapped in your clutter so you can set yourself free. I'm holding the light for you to remember the truth of who you are. I'll guide the way; you just need to take the next step.

LET'S GET REAL TOGETHER

I see you. I know your beauty and power. I know what you're capable of. And my job is to hold the light as you walk home. I won't give up on you. I see you and nothing buried in your clutter can change that.

In this book, I'm going to be vulnerable and real. I am going to share my journey with you. Because I don't value leading from on high. I value walking the path with you. I am asking you do to something brave and life-changing. I know that I need to have some skin in the game if I'm going to ask you to join me. I'm not only going to share my wins. I'm going to share my pain, struggles, and the path I took through the pain. Because I know that together we can find our way out. I want you to feel safe with me, so I will start by being vulnerable with you.

There are possessions in my life that shake me to my core, and I know you have the same. We'll explore them together.

THIS IS MY LOVE LETTER TO YOU

I know that you have a lot of past experience with organizing that didn't go well. And I know you are concerned that this will be another failed attempt. And I know for sure it won't be. This book explains why you've failed to get organized in the past and what to do about it. The truth is that only six things are standing in the way of you getting organized:

- Lack of organizing know-how
- Your inner critic draining your energy
- Uncomfortable feelings that derail you when you're organizing
- Blocks in specific areas of your life
- Negative patterns that show up through your clutter
- Using clutter to get your needs met

As you charge into each chapter, I'm going to show you how these things are keeping you stuck. And then you'll discover what to do about it. I don't want you to leave this book with a long list of tasks and to-dos but a few simple, meaningful actions that will change how you live your life and manage your clutter. Plus, I'm going to share how to keep yourself from backsliding into chaos and clutter again.

THE MISSING LINK TO GETTING ORGANIZED

In the next seven chapters, I'm going to introduce the things that might be keeping you stuck in clutter and chaos.

First, I'm going to teach you the organizing ABCs to make sure you aren't missing a step when it comes to getting organized. Most of us were never taught how to get organized, so learning these basic steps will take the uncertainty and anxiety away from organizing. You will know that you've got the skills to organize anything you come across.

Next, we'll make sure you're not making this process harder than it needs to be. It's super common to think that you're the reason you've got an issue with clutter and chaos, or that there's something wrong with you and you're just not capable of getting organized. I'm going to show you how that's not the case and what you can do to take back your power (and self-esteem). As long as you're blaming yourself, you're missing the truth that's buried in the clutter.

Then we'll move onto the number-one block to getting organized – uncomfortable feelings. Dealing with uncomfortable feelings is probably the most challenging part of organizing, but it's also a necessary evil. There's no world where clutter doesn't bring up big ole' feelings. It's part of the process, but it doesn't have to wreck you. I'll teach you what to do when these uncomfortable feelings rear their heads, so you never get derailed again.

After that, you'll discover how clutter in certain areas of your home points to a block you may be experiencing in a specific area of your life. Knowing what each room means and how it connects to the areas of your life will let you know when clutter is showing you that you're a bit out of balance in your life. Knowing this will put you back in the driver's seat and out of being a victim to clutter.

And speaking of clutter, it's time to learn that clutter isn't random. Once you discover the message hiding in your mess, you will turn clutter into your superpower. You'll learn that you can actually use clutter wisdom to set yourself free from negative patterns in your life.

Then you'll learn how clutter often helps us get our needs met. As long as clutter is helping you out in some way, it's not going to disappear. So, we have to discover how it's trying to help you so you can get that need met in a non-clutter way. Once you do that, the clutter will go away so much more easily because you won't be unconsciously holding it in place to help you get your needs met.

And finally, we'll explore the ways you can make sure that this isn't another failed attempt at getting organized. These unique keys will keep you from backsliding and winding up defeated and feeling overwhelmed and helpless all over again. There's no need for that!

HOW TO READ THIS BOOK

I want you to read this book from front to back once. Once you've read the whole book once, then go back and either use it as a reference as you need it or revisit sections that you think you need more help with. The first time through, don't feel like you need to take action or answer the questions I pose. Allow yourself to digest the information. I'm introducing concepts you've never thought of before and I want you to just entertain the idea that clutter can be seen in a new way. If all you do is plant the seed of this new information in your mind, I consider that a win.

There are things I'll talk about here that you won't think you need. Pay attention to that feeling. Often the things we don't think we need are the things we need most. It's common that the chapter you least want to read is the one you need the most. So, read them all, and then go back and spend more time in any section that calls you. When you get triggered, set the book down for a minute, take three deep breaths, and then keep going. Don't let shame, fear, and other uncomfortable feelings derail you. These insights will guide you home.

TURNING INSIGHT INTO ACTION

At the end of each chapter, you'll find a section called "Turning Insight into Action." These sections will help you take what you've learned and apply it to your life right now. You may feel inspired to do the activity right away. Or you may want to wait until you've read the entire book before taking action. Trust your instincts. You know what's best for you. There are no hard, fast rules here, only guidance meant to support you in your own journey for healing through your clutter.

WHEN ORGANIZING CALLS

As you read, you may feel inspired to put down the book and do some organizing. Go for it! This may be the perfect time to dig in and make big changes. However, it's also possible that you'll start a project and get derailed again. This is not a failure. This is progress. Pick up the book and keep reading. The thing that is keeping you stuck may be the next thing you read.

Pay attention to why you want to organize when you feel that impulse. Were you feeling the need to see some results? Feeling anxious and behind? Maybe you had an ulterior motive. Perhaps you wanted to do it for someone else. Maybe you needed a dopamine hit. There's no judgment, just be aware of your motivation in taking action. That can tell us a lot about why things work, and why they may not be going the way you want.

Also, pay attention to where you felt derailed as you moved through your project. When did you feel overwhelmed, hopeless, or frustrated? Was it a time thing? Did you need something you didn't have? Is this a common pattern for you? We're in the process of making you a clutter detective, all of this is important information. Finishing a project is less important than seeing the evidence you'll discover as you work on projects (successful or not).

WHEN SHAME SHOWS UP

Shame is often a companion on the journey of decluttering. When we feel shame, we often believe that it's true, and then go down a shame spiral. Shame is the dirty little secret that clutter hides inside of you. Feeling shame poisons us from the inside. It makes us question ourselves and our worth. It makes us ignore all the magical, amazing things that we've done and only seek out the negative things that need to change. Shame is the birthplace of perfectionism, and between the two of them, we end up frozen and stuck in place. What if, instead, you saw shame as an alarm that lets you know when you're close to something that needs attention or love?

When we're organizing, there are only two actions that occur. We either embrace something more deeply into our lives, or we release it from our lives. The discomfort comes from standing in between those decisions. World renown tenor, Luciano Pavarotti's father said "… if you try to sit on two chairs, you will fall between them … you must choose one chair." And so it is with our stuff. We must choose to embrace or release the things in our lives. We can't do both. Shame is an alarm that goes off when you're getting close to something you need to embrace or release. It helps you see a decision is at hand.

In *Atlas of the Heart*, Brené Brown says, "Shame thrives on secrecy, silence, and judgment. Shame needs you to believe that you're alone. The antidote to shame is empathy. If we reach out and share our shame experience with someone who responds with empathy, shame dissipates." This is why the role of an organizer is so healing. I can't tell you how many times someone has said to me "I can't believe I have to pay you to listen to my stories about my stuff." Telling your stories, being seen, is a huge part of the healing journey of clutter.

Look, it's natural to look at what's wrong. It's very much human. But that will lead you to seeing more of what's wrong. When you find yourself looking for what's wrong, take a minute to find something that is working well. If I was there with you, I would be looking for what's working well and building on that – not the other way around. There's always something that's working, and you are no exception to that. If your perfectionism, shame, and anger get in the way and say, "no it isn't, everything is total crap," please know that's not the truth. That's a feeling. You've got to feel the feeling, and then go back to looking for what's working. As a clutter detective, you are looking for evidence, not punishment.

WHAT YOUR LIFE WILL LOOK LIKE

As you reframe the way you look at your clutter, you're going to experience a deep sense of freedom. Before, you were trying to get organized based on everyone else's expert solutions. But they left out a very important missing piece – you. You're unique and there are things that your clutter is trying to help you understand. Dealing with clutter is like peeling an onion. Each layer brings you closer to the truth. Your truth. And until you start to see this, getting organized will be like a pot of gold at the end of the rainbow – a fantasy that's just out of reach.

Following the insights shared in this book, you'll start to discover how to tackle clutter from the inside out based on your truth and unique needs. Doing this makes you impervious to clutter. Imagine a world where clutter will never bring you down again because you have tools that work no matter what phase of clutter you're in. That's what this book is offering you. Tools to create your own freedom, no matter what life throws at you.

SUCCESS STORIES

You'll join the many fellow badasses who used their clutter to springboard into fulfilling lives. James transformed his bedroom clutter and welcomed the love of his life. Trish turned a broken teacup into a new purpose and path in life. Charmaine used a photo to awaken a long-lost passion. Your clutter can do the same for you. Let's dig in and discover how to get you unstuck from your clutter and back into your power (where you belong).

Please know that I'll be telling lots of clutter stories here. The names and details have been changed to protect people's privacy. If you read anything and think I'm talking about you, know that's perfectly normal. I can't tell you how many people have almost identical stories when it comes to their clutter, thought patterns and history. You're not alone and there is deep healing that happens as we stand in our truth and start to heal together.

YOU'RE IN THE RIGHT PLACE

You're on the path to getting organized. And I know you may not feel that way right now. But the fact that you found this book means that you're ready for the next level of clutter insight and that you're ready to put clutter behind you. This path is not for the weak of heart. It's a path that can feel intense and overwhelming at times. But you're ready for it. You wouldn't be here unless you were.

This path will not kill you. It might release an old version of you that you no longer need, and it will birth the you that has been in the process of becoming for a long time. Everything you've learned has brought you here. And you're ready for this. You're not starting from scratch; we're building on everything you've ever known and experienced. We're building, not destroying. And you're ready for this. In fact, you've never been more ready.

There will be times you question yourself. That's a very normal thing to do. Questioning yourself makes you human, it isn't proof of your defects. In fact, it's a powerful strength to reflect on things we can improve. So, when you face challenges, know that you're growing stronger. I want you to remember this as you move forward. As you dig into the chapters of this book, I want you to know that this path is divinely laid out before you. You're meant to be here right now reading this book. And the chapters ahead are meant to guide you home. You don't need to struggle alone anymore. Welcome home, my friend.

4

AWAKEN YOUR ORGANIZING GENIUS

Luna and Troy had been trying to get organized for years. Each time they started, they would make progress, get overwhelmed, and then walk away. At a certain point, Luna wondered if she was just genetically unable to organize. Maybe her brain didn't work that way? She and Troy took my Ten Steps to (Finally) Get and Stay Organized Class. Once they knew the steps, it was like being given the key to getting organized in every area of their home. They would no longer get overwhelmed mid-project or feel like they didn't know what they were doing. And when their son, Blaze, needed to organize his desk during summer break, they taught him the Ten Steps and he was able to get organized in no time. In fact, he still uses them to this day. Having a system for getting organized is a powerful skill that will completely change your home and life. Luna and Troy were able to get organized, but more importantly, they were able to make sure that Blaze didn't struggle with clutter the way they had.

AWAKEN YOUR ORGANIZING GENIUS

It's time to awaken your organizing genius! I'm going to go out on a limb here and guess that no one ever taught you how to get organized, or maybe they did, but not for how *your* brain works. You may know the quadratic formula or all the steps in photosynthesis, but you were probably never taught how to organize your stuff.

Maybe you had a caretaker who had no idea how to organize their own clutter and couldn't teach you. Or maybe they were the Martha Stewart of your neighborhood – but they were a total control freak about it and completely disinterested in sharing that information with you because they wanted their house to look like a magazine cover. Thank you, 1950s housewives!

I want to teach you how to organize at the beginning of our journey together because it's really important that you know how to organize. If you don't know how to organize, you won't be able to see the deeper message in your mess. As long as you think clutter exists because of a lack of organizing knowledge, you won't be able to extract the gifts that are buried in your chaos.

MAKE ME A PROMISE

Okay, I *want* to teach you how to get organized. And I can teach you the ten steps that will work every time. BUT, if I teach you these steps, I need you to make me a promise (I know this is a little one-sided because of the whole "this is a book" thing). But this is super, really, annoyingly, completely, totally important. You have to promise me that if you read this chapter and learn all the magical steps to getting organized (that together will work every time), that you will *keep reading this book*. Look, if knowing how to organize was enough, clutter wouldn't exist. This is not new information, organizers like me have been teaching this for over forty years. If organizing know-how was enough, these techniques would have revolutionized the world, and the whole organizing industry would have collapsed because the information is now "out there," and we would no longer have clutter. But sadly, even in spite of this information being out in the world, clutter is growing at a record pace.

Unfortunately, knowing how to organize is one teeny, tiny step in the process of making your clutter go away. When you have recurring clutter, the "how" of getting organized just isn't enough. It will help, but it isn't going to keep it from coming back – that's where the rest of the book comes in. So, if I teach you how to organize, will you do me a solid and keep reading? I promise, I have your best interest at heart. I want this time to be the last time, and just organizing won't solve that. *But* it is super important for you to know how to do it. These steps will be the guide that walk you through the haunted forest. But they won't necessarily stop you from ending up here again. I can show you how to organize but know that everything else in this book will change your life and make you impervious to the clutter of the world. I promise you, it's worth it.

THE SIMPLE SIDE OF ORGANIZING

Lucky for you, the actual process of organizing is a really simple thing. Clutter is an overabundance of stuff in our spaces. If we have an overabundance of stuff in our spaces, what are our options? Well, option one is we reduce the volume of stuff that we have. Option two is we increase the amount of space used to hold that stuff. So, there we go. Clutter solved! Yay! Close this book and walk away because we're done. Drop the mic. Okay maybe not. If it was really that simple, I wouldn't have a job, the organizing industry wouldn't exist, and you wouldn't be on your twenty-seventh round of attempting to figure out why the hell your kitchen counter clutter won't go away.

Organizing is simple. It's not always easy, but it's simple. To break it down, I'm going to teach you my Ten Steps to Get (and Stay) Organized. (Go to http://www.starhansen.com/10stepschecklist if you want a printable guide.) My hope in teaching you these ten steps is that it will awaken your organizing genius. Yes, you've got an organizing genius (and no, my friend, you aren't the exception). Many of these steps will leave you saying, "oh, yeah…I totally knew that." But some will be new and fresh to you. So, take what you need and build on what you've already got!

For the sake of simplicity, we're going to use an example to demonstrate the ten steps. We'll be using a simple, yet juicy area of your home. A space that you access constantly but where you pretty much never want a stranger to go rifling through – your nightstand! This space will be our example and will give you context to understand the process, plus it will be an easy, quick win for you to practice in your own home.

STEP 1 – SET YOUR INTENTION

If you're going on a road trip, how far are you going to go if you have no idea where you're going? Not very far, my friend, not very far. What we need to do is set our intention so we can see this project through to the end. We do that by asking three simple questions:

- What activities will you do in this space?
- How do you want this space to feel?
- How do you want this space to look?

What Activities Will You Do in This Space?

Choose three to five activities you will do in this space. This answer will set the tone for what you will keep in this space and how you will spend time here. I like to limit it to three to five activities because more than that becomes overwhelming. We don't want to create a home of "hopes" but a life well-lived. Less focal points allow us to do more with what we have. For our nightstand example, you might choose the following:

1. Sleep prep (ear plugs, sleep mask, CPAP, etc.)
2. Reading
3. Sexy time gear (toys, lotions, candles, books, restraints – to each their own)
4. Beauty routine (hand lotion, essential oils, etc.)

How Do You Want This Space to Feel?

How do you want to feel when you use this area? If you're not a feelings person, you may want to ask yourself instead, "What do you want to experience here?" This gives you clarity about the state of mind you want to be in while in this area. For your nightstand, you might say:

1. Peaceful
2. Relaxed
3. Comfortable

How Do You Want This Space to Look?

This question lets you get clear about how you would like the aesthetics to shine through here. How you want your personality, values, and creativity to be present. For the nightstand example, we might say:

1. Organized
2. Like a spa
3. Cozy library vibes

These three questions will be your map home. They will stop you from going off the rails and getting pressured to keep too much, or to keep things that don't align with what you want. When in doubt, refer to your answers to these questions and they will tell you whether the items you're debating match up with your intentions. If they do, they can stay. If they don't, they belong somewhere else in the house (or to someone else in the world).

STEP 2 – COLLECT YOUR TOOLS

When we start to organize but don't have our tools prepped and ready to go; we waste a lot of time and allow ourselves to get super distracted as we go around collecting supplies that we need one-by-one. Our brain loves to avoid chaos and will look for any excuse to walk away from organizing and take on a new, more fun project, or to avoid the organizing project completely. It's far better if you have your organizing tools collected and in one place before you begin. In fact, I suggest creating an organizing toolkit that's assembled and ready to organize anytime you are. Here are a few items I like to have on hand when I'm organizing a space:

Tools

- Battery tester (this inexpensive little guy seems 100 percent silly and unnecessary, but trust me, you will wonder how you ever lived without it)
- Box cutter
- Cable ties (Velcro or zip ties)
- Hammer
- Painter's tape (used to mark out furniture and artwork layouts temporarily without damaging your walls)
- Picture hangers
- Post-It's
- Screwdriver
- Tape
- Tape measure (standard and laser style are both great to have)
- Writing Utensils – pen, pencil, Sharpie

Labeling

- Label maker
- Label remover or tweezers (if you've got fingernails you want to protect)
- Label tape
- Scissors

Bags

- Donation bag
- Recycling bag
- Shred bag
- Trash bag
- Ziploc bags (assorted sizes)

Boxes

- Sorting boxes (to contain your categories as you sort)
- Transport boxes (to shuttle things to other rooms in the house)

Self-Care

- Snacks
- Timer or phone (on airplane mode) for breaks
- Water

STEP 3 – DECONSTRUCT

You've done your prep work and it's time to dig in! At the highest level, this step is where you will take everything out of the area that you're working on and sort it into broad categories in a neutral space. When I say a "neutral space" I mean an area that is clear of clutter and allows you to spread out and work on your project in peace. This may be another room in your home, a folding table, or even part of a nearby countertop. Working in a neutral space has many benefits. It allows you to think more clearly, not feel as attached to keeping things because it's where "they've always been," and helps you avoid getting lost in other objects that aren't part of your project.

If you don't have the option of using a completely open neutral space to work in, take a few minutes to clear a space to work. It doesn't have to be perfect. You can put cluttered items from your floor, countertop, or bed into a laundry basket or box while you work in that space, then spread them back out again when you're done. Remember, we're striving for movement over perfection here. I know it can feel overwhelming when every surface feels covered, but I promise there is a solution there: look for possibilities instead of barricades.

Working in a neutral location is something you may want to ignore for convenience and in order to save time. But working in a neutral space makes the difference between feeling completely overwhelmed and lost in the chaos and feeling empowered and capable of tackling the project ahead of you.

First, decide where your neutral location will be. For our sample project, we'll be using the bed. Make sure you clear off anything from the bed that isn't related to the project, so you've got a clear workspace. Next, you're going to remove everything from the nightstand, and put it into broad categories *as* you move them to the bed. It's super important that you don't dump everything into a huge pile on the bed and then try to sort things out. That's a recipe for overwhelm. Instead, create categories as you go: books, sleep gear, lotions, paperwork, etc.

Rooms normally have between five to twenty-five broad categories in them. You don't want to overwhelm yourself with granular categories. So, create broad categories that you can later sub-categorize. For example, create a general office supply category instead of breaking those items down into pens, paper clips, printer cartridges, etc. In the next step, you'll be able to create sub-categories, if needed.

Don't make decisions at this point. Look at everything you touch with neutral eyes, like you're helping a friend get organized and none of this means anything to you. The more neutral you are, the easier this process will be. I promise, there will be plenty of time later for you to make decisions and explore things with more curiosity.

STEP 4 – EVALUATE

To keep? To donate? To store for another ten years in a box at the back of the closet behind your prom dress? It's time to make some decisions! The evaluation step is when you look at each item and decide if you want to keep it, and where it fits into your life now.

For this step, you will look at the items in each category and decide what you'll do with them. Here are a few potential things you might choose to do:

- Keep it and organize it in the current space
- Move it to another room or location
- Trash
- Recycle
- Hazardous waste or electronic recycling
- Donate
- Sell
- Give back to someone else
- Take action (move to your to-do area)

A few suggestions as you evaluate these categories. If your categories feel too big or complicated for you, create sub-categories. Keep breaking categories down into smaller categories until you feel clarity around what you're looking at and what you want to do with the items. Categories are magical and can help create such powerful clarity as you work.

Work through categories from easiest to hardest. Look at the categories you've created and start with the easiest first. Then move onto the next easiest category. Keep going until you've gone through all the categories. Eventually, the hardest category will be the "next easiest category," plus your brain will be warmed up and in organizing mode so it won't feel as hard as it would if you tried to start with the hardest one first.

Make time for your emotions. This is the phase when you need to tell your stories, process feelings that arise, or take a stroll down memory lane. This is literally the time to do that. Don't make yourself rush past this phase; it's super important to the process of organizing and makes the biggest difference when it comes to whether or not your progress will be long-term.

STEP 5 – LET GO

By now you're looking at piles of things that you're going to keep and organize in the current space, as well as bags of donations, trash, recycling, shredding, etc. So, it's time to make space. By getting discarded items out of here, you give yourself more clarity and open space to work.

Take all items that are going elsewhere to their new homes (trash, recycling, etc.) or as close as you can get to their new home. Put donations either in your car or by the door so it's easy to take them away when you leave the house next. If something goes into another room of the house, put it in its new home, or as close as you can get to its new home. It's super important that you not start any new projects during this step. If you found cookbooks by your nightstand that belong in the kitchen, but your cookbook section is already overflowing, don't start to organize the cookbooks in the kitchen to make space for the other books. Put the books as close to their new home as possible and then create a reminder for yourself that you've got a future organizing project with cookbooks in the kitchen.

Because I focus on whole-home, whole-life organizing, I have an important rule of thumb. Whatever space you organize becomes a sacred space. This area needs to be honored and kept organized. All other spaces that haven't been organized yet are fair game. Clutter away! This is a marathon not a sprint. Things don't need to be perfect or done yesterday. By not splintering off into new projects, you keep yourself focused and avoid turning one organizing project into five new endeavors.

STEP 6 – CLEANSE THE SPACE

Now that you've removed the items you're not keeping in this space, it's the perfect time to clean the space. Grab your duster and mop – it's time to freshen the space up. In addition to cleaning the physical space, you can also choose to use this time to do some light renovations (paint, etc.). It's also a great time to do energy clearing if that's something you're into. Meditate in the space to set an intention, put gemstones around the room to help boost certain energetic properties you would like to experience more of, use aromatherapy, or if it's part of your cultural practices, you may want to smudge the space.

STEP 7 – SET UP SOLUTIONS

Congratulations! You've made it to the step where we actually get to organize. Yay!! Isn't it wild that out of the ten steps, only one is actually about what we commonly talk about as organizing? Just one of ten steps. I punctuate this because I want you to know how vital the other steps are to the process of making organizing systems work. The actual process of organizing is small in relation to the other steps and requires the other nine steps to truly be successful.

For this step, you're going to be bringing items from

your "neutral" workspace, back to the space you're organizing as you create these systems. You'll be working primarily in the space you're organizing in order to start exploring solutions. There are four essential guidelines to help you establish successful organizing solutions: categorize, contain, label, and house.

Categorize

Categories give us clarity. Build categories to help you find what you need when you need it. Organizing isn't about putting things away so your house looks nice (although that's a great benefit). Organizing is about putting things away so you can find them when you need them – easily and efficiently. Create categories that help you feel supported by your spaces, are easy to access, and leave you feeling clear about what you have and where it is.

Contain

Put loose items you're keeping into some kind of permanent container. Containers give your stuff physical boundaries. Organizing is nothing if not creating boundaries in our lives. Containers define categories, make them easy to access, and give items a permanent home. Your containers may be plastic bins, decorative baskets, empty shipping boxes, or simply a defined area on a shelf or in a drawer. You will want to use solutions that work best for your brain, aesthetic, and functionality.

Allow for perfect imperfection here. If you don't have a budget for your ideal containers, use some sort of temporary system to maintain your categories (i.e., shipping boxes or grocery bags). I would rather have your categories stay protected while you look for ideal solutions over time, than have you put off completing the project because you can't find the perfect type of container you have in your mind. Done is better than perfect every time!

As you put items into containers to be stored in the area you're organizing, make sure to only fill your containers and drawers to about 80 percent full. You want space to "think inside the box." Ideally, you will be able to dig around inside the box (or drawers) a little bit to find what you're looking for without having to take anything out (thinking "inside the box"). If you have to take things out of the box to find what you need, there's too much in there and you run the risk of creating a whole new project of putting things away once you find what you need. Once the box is 90 percent full, start discarding items as you bring new items in. The old "one in, one out" rule. For each new thing you bring in, eliminate an old one. Or if you're really into paring down, get rid of two things for each new item you add.

Label

Today, you know exactly what your systems mean and what they contain. But Future You will have no idea what your categories mean in three months. Labeling your containers, drawers, and shelves with the name of their category will give you clarity so you always know what you've got. If you're using boxes, I recommend labeling all four sides of the box so that no matter how it gets put away you can always see the label. This can feel super annoying and unnecessary when you're doing it, but it's totally worth it later when your boxes have been shuffled around. I promise, you don't want to learn this lesson the hard way when there's a box you can't reach and there's nothing written on the side of it. Labeling seems like an extra step sometimes, but it protects your categories, helps you be more efficient, and lets everyone in the house know where things are.

House

This part is all about creating a permanent home for your stuff. When it comes to deciding where things will be housed, there are a few things to keep in mind:

- Put things away according to where you will look for them. Ask yourself "Where is the first place I would look for this?" and then put it there. We've all had that moment where we moved our silverware tray and then spent the next six months still opening that old silverware drawer, even though we know they aren't there anymore.
- Keep items in a location close to where they will be used.
- Remember to make items accessible to anyone in the house who will need to use them. Don't store kids' snacks five feet up in the pantry if you need your five-year-old to be able to grab them when they're hungry.
- Always try to minimize the number of steps it takes to access an item. The easier it is to get to (and put away), the greater the chance is that the system will work for you long-term.
- If you need to put things away in a closet or location where you can't easily see what's in there, consider making an inventory and posting it on the door so you can easily see what's stored there. This may feel like overkill to you, or this may be the missing link to staying organized;

always follow your intuition and lean into what works for you.

Back to our nightstand example. We want to make sure that the items you keep here don't just get thrown into your nightstand drawers and instantly become cluttered. As you look at the nightstand items on the bed (your neutral space), observe the categories you've created. For this example, we've got the following categories: sleep prep, reading, sexy time gear, and beauty routine items. Start to think about how you want to store these items so that you have what you need when you need it. Bring the categories from the neutral space into your nightstand one at a time. You're going to create a permanent home for everything. We may stack the books along the bottom shelf of the nightstand; this gives us a clear idea of how many books we have space to keep here. The sexy time stuff may be housed in a small plastic box and stored under a scarf in the lower drawer (so that it stays dust-free and isn't readily available for anyone to see if they come exploring). The top drawer can house daily use items – sleep prep item and your beauty routine. You might let the lotions lay flat in the drawer but want to have some sort of container for the sleep prep items (sleep mask, ear plugs, etc.) so they don't get lost. You might choose a sleek bamboo drawer organizer, or a small, sturdy open box (for easy access). Then, you'll label anything that feels important to you. You might label the inside lip of the drawer where lotions or sleep prep items belong. The sexy time box may not get labeled at all (for privacy), or it may get labeled with a fake code word to keep private things private. Now every category has a home, is contained, labeled and ready for use!

STEP 8 – CREATE YOUR MAINTENANCE PLAN

When it comes to maintaining your organizing systems, flexibility is key. Here are a few keys to making sure your systems stay organized:

- Build systems according to your own unique needs – your energy rhythms, schedule, motivating factors, space, and time. Set up your systems in ways that serve how you naturally think and behave based on your own skills and preferences.
- Piggy-back maintenance routines onto existing systems by building new systems onto existing habits, whenever possible.
- Create your systems and maintenance activities for your laziest day. We are all incredible powerhouses when we're well-rested, nourished, and happy, but how can you actually maintain your systems if you are sick, sad, busy, or overwhelmed? Set your plan up so that even on rough days you can maintain them.
- Cut yourself some slack and avoid perfectionism. Aim for keeping up with 80 percent of your maintenance plan. Life happens. If you get too busy and you have to miss some maintenance, don't stress out about it. Many people miss a maintenance task then beat themselves up and spiral downward quickly – much like a dieter who cheats by having a bite of cake at a birthday party, and then goes home and has a full-on binge because they weren't perfect. If you miss a maintenance task, just jump right back on board the next day.

- Be honest about what you will and won't do. Own your own truth.
- Schedule regular system overhaul sessions with yourself. Even looking at one room a month over the course of a year will ensure that your systems are set up for success to support you. We do this in the Chaos to Calm Community (my online organizing community) and it is a total game-changer when it comes to evolving your organizing systems.
- There is no "done." Your systems, like you, are constantly evolving and growing. Edit systems when you see they're not working for you. You, your spaces, and your routines will always have an element of change present. There is no such thing as being done when it comes to organizing because you are always changing and growing. You are not static, and neither is your stuff, systems, or space.
- If there is a breakdown in the system, get curious. Let system dysfunctions be an invitation to evolve the system, not to beat yourself up. Look for clues. What is working well? What is not working? Make adjustments to the systems to more optimally support yourself.

For the nightstand project, you may establish a maintenance rule that every night the surface of your nightstand has to be clear. Or maybe you only want to do that once a week. It's up to you! Watch for red flags that illuminate breakdowns in the system, such as random piles of trash appearing on the nightstand or the floor. If things start piling up, ask yourself what the mess is showing you that you need. In this case, the system breakdowns may be showing that we need a trash can next to the nightstand. By getting curious instead of beating yourself up when things get a little messy, you learn to evolve your systems and keep your nightstand (and rooms) organized, all while learning to trust that you are capable of getting (and staying) organized.

STEP 9 – BEAUTIFY

I bet you thought we were done! Not yet, my friend. Before we can call a space organized, we need to make it pretty! Beautifying a space isn't about making it look nice for other people (though that can be a plus if it feels good to you). It's about you expressing your true essence into the spaces of your home. So that when you look at the spaces you've organized, you feel like you see yourself there.

When we feel happy with and find a space beautiful, we're more likely to avoid cluttering it or using it as a dumping ground. So, get out those photos, track down that statue you love and make the spaces you organize look beautiful. I even love to decorate inside closets and cabinets with decorative accents. I have my great-grandmother's artwork inside my pantry. It feels like she is winking at me every time I go in there. Take time to infuse your life, personality, and joy into the spaces of your home.

STEP 10 – CELEBRATE

Done? Almost! The last stop on our organizing tour is for you to celebrate your amazing hard work. Too often we do lots of amazing things in our lives but then just keep on living like nothing special happened. Every time you make progress with your organizing, something special happened, and it needs to be celebrated! I recommend making a list of things you can do to celebrate. List anything you can think of, from free and easy things you can do at home right now, all the way to high-end splurge celebrations. Choosing your reward before you start organizing can really help you stay motivated. Please note, that depending on how your brain is wired, you may need to celebrate *before* you start working or as you start working (I have a client who needs to have a can of her favorite sparkling water and dance music blaring before she is able to get into the organizing zone). Lean into what works best for you!

TURN INSIGHT INTO ACTION

Now that you know how to organize a space, I want you to practice. The more you do it, the easier it will be and the better you'll get. You want to start small. I can't tell you how many people get burned out because they decide to tackle their whole garage + car trunk + gardening shed + back porch in a single weekend. You want to start small and build up to a whole room. I recommend starting with what I call Small Zones (junk drawer, purse, bathroom drawer, car console, shower, kitchen utensils, plastic shopping bags, etc.). These areas should take you thirty minutes or less. Once you feel strong organizing a Small Zone, move to Medium Zones (kitchen cabinet, under the kitchen sink, coffee table, etc.). Medium Zones should take about an hour to complete. Once you feel confident with Medium Zones, move to Large Zones (linen closet, pantry, entertainment center, refrigerator, bookshelf). These zones will take you two to six hours to complete. Once you feel solid with Large Zones, you're free to start working on whole rooms. But always work your way up. This is a marathon, not a sprint.

Remember, organizing is a skill you're cultivating in your life. Once you have this skill, no one can take it away from you and you can apply it to any size project. These steps are the same ones I use if I'm organizing a junk drawer, or a three-car garage stacked to the ceiling.

The other skill we're refining in your life is completion. So often we start organizing but get lost along the way and never finish. Working your way up from Small Zones allows you to experience the very healing process of completion. It helps you learn to trust yourself, solidify your skills, and strengthen the skill of completion.

Bonus Tip

A word to the wise, try to save paperwork and emotionally charged items for later. Emotionally charged items might include memorabilia, unresolved paperwork projects, things you have no idea what to do with, or items that bring up a lot of shame or grief. These items are usually "burning a hole in our pocket" and we want to get them done yesterday. But I promise, you will be much better served if you wait until you feel confident with the process of organizing first (and until you've read further along in the book). I promise we'll get you there, but first things first.

5

WHY ORGANIZING DRAINS YOUR ENERGY

"The curious paradox is that when I accept myself exactly as I am, then I am able to change."

— CARL ROGERS

Congratulations, you now know everything that I know from two decades of getting people organized. You're a lean, mean, organizing machine! It may take you a hot minute to really internalize the steps covered in Chapter 4, but you now have the skills to tackle any organizing project that crosses your path.

Getting confident with using these steps is essential to getting organized. This wisdom becomes a power that sets you free and allows you to see the true reason for your clutter not going away. As long as you think you've got an organizing problem, you're going to miss out on the real truth your clutter is trying to tell you. Feeling like we don't know how to get organized is a crutch that keeps us from seeing the truth hiding in our clutter. Now that you know how to organize, you're ready to go deeper. So, keep reading and let's set you free from the things that have been keeping clutter stuck in your life.

THE BLAME GAME

Dionne, just like you, is a badass. She is a successful lawyer who put herself through school, built a thriving practice, and now resides on the coast of California. She owns a beautiful home with a breathtaking view and spends her off days adventuring with her hunky hubby and their fur babies. From the outside, her life looks perfect. But several decades into her career, the death of her mom and extreme burnout have led her to feel swallowed whole by the clutter. She is successful in so many areas of her life, and there have been many times when she has felt organized. She knows she must have been even somewhat organized to successfully make it through so many years of school. But she can hardly even remember that. Her entire home is absolutely drowning in items from her parent's home, countertops are overflowing with paperwork, closets are bursting at the seams with four different sizes of clothing, and her kitchen pantry is overflowing into the garage and basement. She wants to get organized. She *needs* to get organized. But every time she tries, she ends up sitting in front of the TV with either a glass of wine or pint of ice cream. It's like organizing just drains every single ounce of energy she has. So, she beats herself up before she even starts to organize. She beats herself up when she chooses to watch TV over organizing. She beats herself up when she actually does organize but stops because it feels too hard or if she gets distracted. At this point, organizing feels like punishment and it's just too stressful to even want to do it anymore. It's hard not to feel hopeless and fall into a deep shame spiral. She chooses not to even try anymore because, why bother?

When I met with Dionne she was at her wit's ends. We were discussing her paperwork. I asked her why she thought the pile of paper on her kitchen counter kept reappearing no matter what she did. "It's because I'm lazy," she said. I could see by the fierceness in her eyes that she really meant this. "You've put yourself through school, established a strong career, and have a beautiful life and family. None of this sounds like something a lazy person could do."

Blaming ourselves is one of the most human things we do. That inner critic jumps in and starts pointing out everything we're doing wrong and every possible flaw. It's one of the most detrimental things we struggle with when it comes to organizing.

THE ENERGY DRAIN OF ORGANIZING

You know how it goes, you start organizing and suddenly feel exhausted. Or you think about organizing but are suddenly flooded with a desire to do the dishes or flip on the TV.

Why does organizing drain you of your energy – often before you even begin? I'll tell you why. There's a bully in the house. And no, I'm not talking about your spouse, mom, neighbor, or your furry friend in the corner giving you the side eye. I mean you.

The biggest bully we have when it comes to getting organized is ourselves. It's like we're constantly on the hunt for evidence of our defects. Looking relentlessly for what's wrong with us. Not stopping until we find proof that there is, in fact, something wrong with us.

I know life is rough, and so many things feel out of your

control. But I promise, beating up on yourself or thinking the worst of yourself just isn't going to get you organized and it certainly isn't going to set you free from the chaos. That behavior and way of thinking drags you down. It doesn't lift you up. And you deserve to only have things in your life that lift you up, including the way you speak to yourself.

It's easy to look at the clutter and chaos in our lives and determine that we are the common factor that's keeping it in place. Blaming ourselves can feel like a way of taking responsibility for our actions, but it can also be holding you down and keeping you from making significant progress. The surprising truth is that there's actually nothing wrong with you that's causing the clutter (no matter what the voice in your head says). There are countless worries that may be keeping you stuck. You may struggle to trust yourself. You may feel like you have to take on the responsibility of the world around you and think you shouldn't need any help. Or maybe you assume you don't know what you're doing. Perhaps you think there's something wrong with you, that you're defective, or that you're missing the organizing gene. You might also think you're the only one with this issue. No matter which thoughts flood your mind when it comes to your clutter and getting organized, this inner critic is draining your energy. And that energy drain is one of the main reasons why it's hard to get organized.

I don't know about you, but I am not my most effective when someone is beating me down. Imagine this, you've decided to run a marathon. But every time you begin, someone comes up and punches you. Or they trip you. Or they dig a hole for you to fall in somewhere along the way. Would you be very interested in running that marathon once you started to see that pattern of constant attack? Or would it feel too scary or even abusive to begin? That's what it's like when we're organizing. We get started, all hopeful and well-meaning – then beat ourselves up and look for the worst in ourselves. These inner critic negative voices pummel us until even the idea of organizing is just too much to bear. You tell yourself that you're not capable of getting organized. That you don't know what you're doing. You remind yourself of all the missteps in the past. You tell yourself that everyone else knows what they're doing, has it all together, or doesn't struggle the way you do. You convince yourself that you're the worst. Even now, you're probably thinking, "Yeah, Star, but I *am* the worst – you don't even know." Okay, yes I do. And you're not the worst. I can guarantee you that.

So often people talk about feeling overwhelmed when they start to get organized. This inner critic is one of the biggest reasons why. The good news is that this is all within your control. You can choose to redirect that energy and take your power back. The inner critic does not need to drive your organizing projects or your mental state.

Right about now you may want to set this book down. You may feel like this is too much and you don't want to do the work. You want to get organized, so why are we talking about the inner critic? Look, I know this deeper dig can be scary. It confronts things you've worked your whole life to hide. But if you want different results, we have to approach this differently. If you want your external clutter gone, we have to start by evicting your internal clutter. And your inner critic is public enemy number one.

WE'RE WIRED FOR IT

Now, before you go and start blaming yourself for blaming yourself, I want you to stop right there. Humans are biologically built to look for what's wrong. It's how we've stayed alive for as long as we have (it certainly isn't the sharpness of our claws and teeth that did it). We're literally hard-wired to look for what's wrong. Our caveman ancestors needed to constantly be on the lookout for danger and all the many threats that might kill us: lions, poison berries, floods. But the problem is that we no longer need that relentless hypervigilance to keep us alive – yet we still commit to it every day. Every day that you double down on looking for danger in your life, you keep yourself in survival mode. You stress yourself out, keep your nervous system dysregulated, and make yourself less effective. The good news is that you can start to change this anytime you're ready.

It's okay to break up with your inner critic (or at least send it on an extended vacation). You're more important than the stuff. You don't deserve to be punished. If you feel like you've wasted something because you've never used it, holding onto it won't make it less wasteful, it only means you're holding onto trash in your home. And you deserve so much better than that.

If you want peace of mind, you're going to have to pay for it by letting go of your self-criticism and judgment.

Your inner critic was biologically handed down from our ancestors but then perpetuated by circumstances in your life. So far, it has seemed helpful but it's weighing you down. And it is something you can release and live without. In fact, you'll thrive once you let it go. Start simply. When you hear yourself speak ill of or look for the worst in yourself, tell your survival brain, "Thank you for trying to keep me safe. I've got this, you can step back now." And then let your highest-self step in and align with your truth. Take a deep breath and replace that survival statement with something that is more nourishing and encouraging, such as, "I've done hard things before. I can do this."

WHAT IF CLUTTER ISN'T YOUR FAULT?

What if I told you that clutter isn't your fault? Have you been waiting to hear those words? Or do they feel impossible to believe? Look, clutter is complicated. If you're like most people I talk to, you've been living with clutter so long that it's hard to know where it stops, and you begin. It's common to lose ourselves in the clutter. Our inner voice blends with the "noise" of the clutter. Sometimes, it's hard to even be able to breathe around the clutter. We often over-identify with the clutter and may think it's all our fault and that we're defective for having it in our lives. But that simply isn't true. And as long as you act from that train of thought, you're going to stay stuck. The truth is: clutter isn't your fault.

There's so much going on when it comes to clutter – far beyond the high volume of stuff. And as long as you take the blame and keep the cause of the clutter so general, you'll miss out on discovering the message buried in your mess.

It's easy to think you're the only one struggling here, especially with our social feeds flooded with beautiful home "after" pics, decanted pantries, and A-list declutter porn.

But look, you're not alone. This is one of the most common challenges people are dealing with today. And the cause may not be what you think it is. The truth is that there are a lot of forces contributing to your clutter and chaos beyond you having too much stuff or not enough space.

LEARN TO TRUST YOURSELF THROUGH ORGANIZING

Organizing offers you an incredible gift – the ability to trust yourself again. When it comes to getting organized, we look at the graveyard of failed attempts, projects stopped mid-way through, piles of unused organizing solutions, unread books, and the trickle of clutter in every area of the house and car. You might see an over-arching theme there – that you can't trust yourself. If your past experience is indicative of the future, why even bother trying again. And yet, you're holding this book. Something in you knows that there's something else going on. Another path that might get you there. And the truth is that organizing, the thing that seems like the birthplace of failure, is actually the perfect place to learn to trust yourself again. Look, you were never taught how to organize, and the TV shows aren't really teaching you; they're giving you a sample of the after-effects of organizing. Trust me. The one thing that the cameras don't film is the actual organizing process; it's almost more boring to watch than paint drying. But now you know how to get organized. And knowing that frees you to discover the message in your mess, and to see your clutter with new eyes – all things I'm teaching you in this book. With this insight you *can* turn clutter into a path of learning to trust yourself again.

Clutter is an external demonstration of your inner world. As scary as it can feel to believe that there's magic in it being true. Instead of trying to figure out what's wrong with you, you can sort through the clutter and find countless solutions, assets, and answers you never knew you had within you. Clutter allows you to stop looking for answers outside of yourself. The answers are within you and clutter is the key to discovering them. If the challenges are in the clutter, the solutions are buried in there too. We just have to stop hunting for what's wrong and start excavating what's right. It's time to learn to trust yourself again. It's time to come home to yourself. Clutter can get you there. Every time you start and complete a project (no matter how small), you reinforce the truth – that you *can* trust yourself. And when you find things in your clutter that remind you of the badass you are, you reinforce that truth, that you're a fantastic person who deserves good things in life. Allow clutter to walk you home.

PLANTING A SEED OF CHANGE

My wish for you is to have you start to imagine a world where you're not defective and clutter isn't proof that there's something wrong with you. I know we're fighting against a lifetime of you seeking proof of the opposite, so it might take a hot minute (or a lifetime) to get there. But if all you do at this moment is plant a seed that it might be possible, then I know it can grow into something big and beautiful. You can transform the way you look at yourself. You can look at yourself in a way that will lift you up instead of tear you down. And you deserve that in every possible way.

There's no magic wand I can wave that will shift your mindset immediately. But what I can do is plant a seed that there is another way. Let's try something new. Imagine this for a moment, just a moment. What if there's nothing wrong with you? What if clutter is simply here to deliver a message that will change your life for the better?

I'm not asking you to magically turn around a lifetime of blaming yourself and looking for what's wrong. All I want is for you to imagine a world where you're not defective and clutter isn't proof that there's something wrong with you. You've spent a lifetime refining the skill of looking for your defects in the hope that you can save yourself and turn the ship around. But the ship has already turned around, my friend. You are a badass and no amount of perceived proof in the other direction can make anything else true. I know it's scary to put down the sword. I know that under the chaos, blaming, and inner criticism, there is something tender and delicate. And you're afraid of it being destroyed by the challenges of this world. Hummingbirds are delicate and beautiful and seemingly vulnerable. But they are also fierce, powerful, and capable of taking care of themselves. You are the same.

I know this path. I too have battled with my inner critic most of my life. My inner critic tore me down but promised me perfection and control. It told me that if I looked for the worst of myself then I could make changes and be the person I always wanted to be. It promised me perfection, but it delivered abuse.

I don't know about you, but I don't respond well to bullies. And when the bully lives inside of you, it's hard to escape or change your behavior, because from that mindset we'll always be acting out against ourselves.

Control and perfectionism are false illusions. There's no such thing as perfection, and control is a total illusion. We want to "let go" of clutter. But we have to start by letting go of the need for perfectionism and control.

AWAKENING INTUITION

There is a Cherokee story about two wolves. A grandfather tells his grandson about a battle between two wolves inside us all. One is evil. The other good. The grandson asks, "Which wolf wins?" The grandfather replied, "The one that you feed." What we give our attention to grows. We have the ability to grow our inner critic, or to starve it out and give our attention to something else. Something that will create strength, harmony, and clarity within us, no matter the state of our homes, lives, or the world around us. That something is intuition. We've all got it, and the more we use it, the more powerful it becomes. If the inner critic is the enemy of organization, intuition is the fuel that propels it forward.

Intuition is not some airy-fairy concept that is only for people crunching on granola while meditating eight hours a day. In fact, the US Military has invested millions of dollars researching intuition to help their soldiers to respond to situations without consciously analyzing the situation. Every person has intuition. It's physically built into who you are. Intuition is the actual psychological process where the brain uses environmental cues (and past experiences) to make decisions. Now, this process happens so quickly that you may not even notice it's happening, but it is, and it's quite impactful. In fact, it has even been suggested that people's intuition often arrives at better decisions than the part of our brain which makes deliberate decisions. So, the good news is that you have intuition, and it's already happening. Now we just need to learn to hear it and separate it out from the other, less awesome voices in your head.

To get to know your intuition better, let's first explore what intuition doesn't sound or feel like.

- Accusatory
- Attacking
- Brings up the past
- Coercive
- Constantly changes what it says
- Critical

- Highly emotional
- Manipulative
- Minimizes your experience and feelings
- Urgent
- Uses fear, lack, or scarcity
- Clenching or discomfort in your body
- Feelings of uncertainty or anxiety

When you hear thoughts or feel feelings that align with the above list, know that you're probably dealing with the inner critic, ego, wounding, trauma responses, or fear.

Now let's dig into what your intuition *does* sound and feel like.

- Absence of emotion when you receive the insight
- Calm, simple, steady voice (more of a whisper than a scream)
- Consistent – repeats itself gently as many times as you need
- Confident or peaceful about your decision (even if it doesn't make sense to others or isn't logical)
- Lucid dreams
- Stays in the present
- There is no coercion
- Clarity and ease
- Energized
- Inspired and excited to take action
- Light/peaceful physically and mentally
- You have recurring thoughts, ideas, or inspiration (they will keep coming up until you act on them) – especially during more quiet, peaceful times
- You see repeating symbols or patterns around you (objects, music, dreams, numbers, etc.)

- You start to see opportunities appear around you

When you experience these sensations, rest assured that you are in the magical flow of your intuition. From this sense of knowing, you can take powerful action and make decisions that are for your highest good.

TURNING INSIGHT INTO ACTION

So, how do we apply this to the organizing process? Anytime you need to tap into your intuition – whether it be for making decisions about what to discard, making peace with painful situations in your life, or how to get started on a difficult project, you can use the following steps.

How to Hear Your Intuition

- Calm your body and clear your mind
- Take a few deep breaths
- Detach from the outcome – release what you want and be open to what is
- Remind yourself that all humans have intuition, and it is possible for you to hear yours
- Express gratitude for receiving guidance (before you get it)
- Ask a simple, clear question you want guidance around
- Feel for mental guidance and/or sensations in your body (i.e., gut feeling)
- Breathe into and release any negative or critical voices
- Lean into the answers that feel good, grounded, or peaceful

- As you experience something that feels good, grounded, or peaceful, look for the next right action you can take toward that intuitive insight

The more you use your intuition, the stronger it gets. And once you're acting from your intuition, so many things that slow you down and make organizing feel like a painful process will melt away without you even noticing.

As you practice hearing your intuition, you want to lean into the feelings of "yes" that come up for you. But many times, we feel a strong "no." I find that in life when you feel a strong *no*, it's often directing you toward your *yes*. It's not saying "no, never!" It's saying, "not this way, try again." Even if one direction isn't your path, the good news is that you've got 359 other degrees to face and try. One of them will be your yes. And that's what you're looking for – a yes that feels in flow, even if it doesn't make sense to anyone else. You're looking for the direction that feels like there's movement and openness for you.

It's time to put the sword down and stop fighting with yourself. Your inner critic costs way too much to keep them on payroll. Plus, there are so many other great options beyond constantly beating yourself up. It's time to advocate for yourself, trust yourself, and lean into your yes. The answer is within you, and it's time to hear it.

6

MANAGING THE BIG FEELINGS THAT SIDELINE YOU EVERY TIME

"This being human is a guest house
Every moment a new arrival.
A joy, a depression, a meanness,
Some momentary awareness comes
As an unexpected visitor.
Welcome and entertain them all!
Even if they are a crowd of sorrows,
Who violently sweep your house
Empty of its furniture,
Still, treat each guest honorably.
He may be clearing you out
For some new delight.
The dark thought, the shame, the malice.
Meet them at the door laughing and invite them in.
Be grateful for whatever comes.
Because each has been sent
As a guide from beyond."

— RUMI

THE POWER OF STUFF

I look up as Simone floats out of the bathroom. She looks at me and beams a wide, million-dollar smile, "Star!"

The peacock blue of her dress catches my eye. My throat clenches. I can hardly breathe. It feels like someone punched me in the gut as I force my mouth into a smile. I try to awaken a sparkle in my eyes to hide the pain that is pulsing through my body.

"It's your dress!" she says.

I haven't seen that dress in five years. Not since I ripped it off my body while screaming, minutes after learning that my sister took her own life.

I wore that dress to countless parties, weddings, and events. It was my "sisterhood of the traveling dress" with my best friend Penelope, Simone's sister. But after ripping it off my body that day, I asked Pen to go to my house and grab that dress. "I never want to see it again," I said. It reminded me of the moment my life changed forever, and I didn't want to have to come near that moment again for the rest of my life.

But here it was. Staring me down on the most important day of Pen's life. She sat in the rocking chair of her parents' bedroom, moments from walking down the aisle with the love of her life, eight months pregnant and glowing. I couldn't wreck this day for her. No matter what.

I took a deep breath, wrapped my arms around Simone, and said, "You look amazing!"

The day that followed was a whirlwind of choking back emotions and putting on a good face. By the end of the day, I had a paralyzing migraine and was spinning, all from seeing that one dress. That is the power of physical objects.

EMOTIONS ARE A GATEWAY

Emotions are what give physical objects their power. And clutter is a gateway to emotions.

When people say that organizing is easy and we just need to "get to work", this is the understanding that they are so casually missing. The reality is that buried in the clutter are painful feelings just waiting to pounce. The hard truth is that a single object can transport us back into deep grief and completely wreck us.

When we organize, we come across countless items that mean nothing to us. But then there are painful little gems hidden all throughout the clutter. I call these landmines. Those objects can rip us apart with a simple glance. Those objects make us question ourselves and get totally lost in the moment.

Emotions are the number one reason you get derailed when you're organizing. And learning how to face and move through difficult feelings while you're organizing will set you free and give you power you didn't know was possible.

I know you often don't want to feel your feelings. Feelings are the other F- word. Many people would prefer the F-bomb I dropped on the front of this book, rather than the ones that bubble up inside of them while organizing. Lots of feelings feel horrible and I wish that I could wave a magic wand and make them go away. Feelings are the biggest roadblock in organizing, but they're also the biggest gift. If you don't listen to and feel your feelings, they'll just keep getting louder and louder until you finally pay attention to them. Trust me on this – listen to the whisper, don't wait for the scream.

STOP FAKING IT

We live in a world that values "putting on a good face." Many people are overwhelmed in their own lives and the idea of having to hold space for someone else's pain feels like too much. So, we learn to not burden people. We shove our painful feelings down and slap a plastic smile on our face, in the hopes of being accepted, loved, or not too "much" for those we love. This is called Emotional Bypassing. The concept is that we should be happy and doing well all the time. But this just isn't how life works. And every time you choose to bypass what you're feeling to be "happy," you're abandoning yourself. And your body, mind, and spirit will only tolerate being abandoned for so long. It's one of the reasons that organizing feels like it gets more difficult each time. Those feelings that you're trying to avoid are getting louder and more painful because they refuse to go "quietly into the night." They will keep working to get your attention. If you've gotten to a place where you can't even imagine starting to get organized, that might be a major reason why.

I know it can be terrifying to feel our feelings. I remember a year after my sister died, I was holding back grief and fighting the urge to cry because I was 100 percent sure that those feelings would kill me. When I finally couldn't hold back anymore, I cried for forty-five minutes straight. Then, the tears stopped. I took a few deep, raggedy breaths and felt so much better. Those feelings didn't kill me. In fact, holding them off was more painful than actually moving through them. That moment was a game-changer for me.

Emily and Amelia Nagoski wrote a wonderful book called *Burnout*. In it, they say, "Emotions are tunnels. If you go all the way through them, you get to the light at the end. Exhaustion happens when we get stuck in an emotion."

The truth is feelings are not the issue. Avoiding feelings or getting stuck in feelings; those are the things that will hurt you. Through is the only way out.

BURIED PAIN

We spend so much energy burying the things that hurt us. We use food, TV, alcohol, sugar, sex, clutter, shopping, drugs, etc. You name it and there's a coping skill to help you avoid feeling painful emotions. Clutter also helps us hide painful feelings. It's natural to get overwhelmed and not want to organize because clutter often feels like a giant pile of pain.

But buried in that clutter is also deep, profound healing. Organizing carries with it a unique and lasting style of healing that no other modality offers. Organizing is an archeological dig of your heart through your home. The process of organizing brings painful feelings to the surface so you can heal them and release them from your life. And beyond that, you get the experience of moving through difficult feelings and back into gentle, productive action, teaching your body and mind that you are resilient. You can do hard things. And as scary as that may sound, you're trading pain for freedom. You truly can heal and let things go that no longer serve you – both emotionally and physically.

NOTE ABOUT TRAUMA

If you find yourself experiencing numbness, irritability, or fear when confronting something challenging in your life you may be experiencing unresolved trauma or PTSD.

Many people who survived trauma in childhood have difficulty identifying or expressing emotions because they lack an emotional vocabulary. Having an emotional vocabulary means knowing that you're experiencing a feeling, and being able to name the emotion that you're feeling. Without having an emotional vocabulary, feeling emotions or processing through them may feel more complicated or almost impossible to do. If you think you may be experiencing this in your life, I recommend that you get the support of a therapist or practitioner who specializes in trauma. We can't "feel our way" out of trauma and often need more support to find our way through.

THE HEALING POWER OF ORGANIZING

Let's talk about the healing power of organizing. Organizing awakens many big feelings that we may have worked hard to avoid. But, as painful as organizing seems, it's actually a treasure trove of healing and empowerment. Especially when we see it as a practice and not a task to complete. There are so many things in life that we have absolutely no control over. Each day can feel torturous as we look at the world and notice that there is so much we have no power over. We've never had more connection in this world. It's beautiful but can be overwhelming. In a matter of seconds, you can know about every crisis happening across the planet. Humans are not built for that level of information. Dunbar's number is a theory that suggest the human psyche is built to engage with a community of around 150 people in close proximity to us. And now we are in touch with millions across every inch of the globe. It's hard not to be overwhelmed.

Where does organizing fit into healing this sense of overwhelm? Well, organizing can give us a sense of empowerment and control in our lives. By choosing projects and completing them, we allow ourselves a powerful hit of dopamine; the feel-good brain chemical that makes us want to keep moving forward. It doesn't matter if it's completing a whole garage organizing project or just your kitchen junk drawer, your brain gets the same message that progress is being made and it's safe to keep going.

Plus, as you organize the piles in your home, you're given the opportunity to experience closure around unresolved pieces of your life. As challenging as it can feel, while you're organizing, you come across things that need resolution in your life – both emotional and practical. As you confront the items that remind you of the situation, you are given the opportunity to emotionally resolve the situation, and then you physically resolve the object; this solidifies the resolution on a deep level because you're physically seeing changes that match your emotional state.

This inside-out process of making peace with the complicated parts of your life through organization is deeply healing. There's a magic that happens as you rock back and forth between organizing and doing deep emotional work. You become more effective by organizing, and you heal parts of yourself that need healing that you might have forgotten about. As hard as it can be, you're setting yourself free in a multitude of ways. Plus, it's powerful to know that you can physically see and experience a practical difference to match that deep inner healing.

TELL YOUR STORY

As you organize, you may be flooded with memories, insights, and feelings. This is a powerful part of the organizing journey. It's normal to think you don't have time to feel these feelings, tell your story, or process what you uncover. We've learned to be a society of doers who race from one thing to another. But the truth is that the power is in the details. Feelings are a part of organizing, not something unnecessary that has come to distract you. Telling your stories is PART of the organizing process. Feeling big feelings are a huge part of the organizing process. You're not getting distracted and being lazy, you're doing exactly what needs to be done – processing the layers of your clutter.

This is one of the reasons why organizing is such an effective healing activity; it allows you to rock between emotional processing and moving forward. You don't just sit and feel your feelings and then melt into the floor like a blob. You feel your feelings, and then you continue moving forward, just like in life. This practice of being present with what is, leaning into the truth and feelings present, then moving forward is one of the most powerful things you can learn. And organizing is an incredible teacher in this. Clutter holds stories, emotions, freedom, empowerment, and ease. There is magic in your clutter, and it will heal you faster and more deeply than you realize.

MANAGING BIG EMOTIONS WHEN ORGANIZING

Luna was going through an old box of paperwork in her garage when she came across a letter from her mom, who had since passed away. She instantly recognized her handwriting and felt a clench in her stomach. She started to read but suddenly was flooded with emotions. It was hard to breathe and all she wanted to do was put it back, shove the box back on the shelf, and go back to the house. "No way am I doing this right now!" she thought.

Getting triggered by objects comes up quite often when

we're organizing. But sometimes the feelings aren't even that dramatic. Sometimes, it's as subtle as you thinking about organizing and then hearing a voice in your head say, "You're never going to get done – what's the point?" Or you're in the middle of organizing and it feels like it's taking forever and the voice in your head tells you what a loser you are and how no one else has to spend all weekend organizing their stuff. Then it plays "the greatest hits" montage of all the people you know who have "it all together," followed by a highlight reel of all the ways you feel like you don't.

Painful feelings have a way of sneaking in when we least expect it while organizing. It really is the number one thing that will derail you while organizing. So, what can you do about it? Well, there are six steps that will help you handle big feelings when they pop up.

1. Notice something's up
2. Explore it with curiosity
3. Name it
4. Process the feeling
5. Shift
6. Move forward

Let's dig in and explore each step more deeply.

STEP 1 – NOTICE SOMETHING'S UP

The first step is awareness. If you don't want uncomfortable feelings to derail your organizing progress, you've got to know when an uncomfortable feeling is present.

When we feel an uncomfortable feeling, the discomfort doesn't feel good. So, we naturally want to avoid it or escape it. These feelings can also trigger our inner wounded child, who then freaks out that this feeling of discomfort will destroy us or never end. Our brain, body, and psyche, being as smart and powerful as they are, go into action mode, looking for ways to help us escape.

Some people may experience physical signs like tension in their gut, a feeling of agitation, a craving for something sweet and comforting, or an impulse to grab their phone and check their messages. Whatever your signs, they're yours. There is nothing wrong with them. There's nothing wrong with you and how you process life. This is your unique way of dealing with it. We all have our own distinct roadmap for how we avoid pain.

Your body is the gateway to awareness. When you feel signs of discomfort, curiosity will guide you through to the deeper meaning.

The best first step is to become aware of the tension and avoidance patterns in our bodies. Tension and stress are the physical clutter of our bodies, trying to get our attention and help us see something bigger is happening. Take a few deep breaths and scan your body looking for the following sensations, signs and impulses:

Bodily Sensations

- Tight muscles
- Clenched jaw
- Holding your breath
- Panting
- Tightening your fists or toes
- Swallowing hard
- Racing heart rate
- Shaking
- Tunnel vision
- Headache

- Nausea

Mental Signs

- Agitation
- Racing thoughts
- Feeling edgy
- Skin crawling
- Loud noises put you on edge
- Overstimulated
- Feel like silence is deafening
- Restlessness

Impulses to Distract

- Food
- Sugar
- Scrolling
- Social media
- Sex
- Drugs
- Alcohol
- TV
- Venting or blaming
- Escapism – desire to flee
- Impulse to clean
- Workaholism

Once you've discovered the clues alerting you to something bigger going on, it's time to get curious.

STEP 2 – EXPLORE WITH CURIOSITY

It's time to get curious about (and present to) whatever is going on for you. Now that you've noticed that something doesn't feel quite right let's lean in a bit. Instead of shoving the feeling back down, or trying to avoid it, let's explore it instead.

You're going to do this by getting curious about what's present for you at this moment.

Explore the uncomfortable feeling without judgment – judgment of yourself or the feeling. Your psyche may try to jump to judgment. It thinks that focusing on what's wrong will help you; remember, it's how we're wired. But all judgment does is lead you down a rabbit hole and delay you from moving beyond this feeling.

Try not to jump to conclusions or race to take action. Those are standard avoidance techniques. Instead, what we need to do is to become aware of and in touch with your moment-to-moment experience – to be truly present.

Take a few nice deep breaths. Visualize yourself growing roots through your feet into the ground. Feel yourself being held by the earth below you and the air surrounding you. Once you feel grounded and calm, scan your body. Notice any sensations that may be present.

Simply be aware of the sensations you feel. You're showing yourself that it's safe to feel. You're showing the uncomfortable feeling that you're here and listening.

This is a vital step in facing your feelings and showing up for yourself.

Gently explore the following questions:

- What sensations do you feel?
- Where do you feel that in your body?
- Does the sensation move, shift, or drift?

- Are there any thoughts that come with that sensation?
- Do you feel tension anywhere?
- How does your gut feel?
- Is there any tension in your jaw or scalp?
- How is your breathing? (Are you holding your breath? Is it moving with ease, or is it jagged or sped up?)
- Do you feel any urges to escape or distract from this moment?
- Do you feel any thoughts that come with this sensation?
- Do you have any judgment about these sensations or feelings?
- If this feeling had a color, what color would it be?
- What shape best describes it?
- What sound would it make?
- Do you get the sense that this feeling is helping you avoid something uncomfortable?

The more curious you can get the better. Remember, uncomfortable feelings are trying to get your attention. The more you give them your love and attention, the less painful or chaotic they need to be to get your attention. The less you hide those feelings, the less you'll need clutter to mask them. This can feel scary, but you are capable of hard things and deserve taking this time to heal.

STEP 3 – NAME IT

Now that you're in touch with the sensation let's try to name it. It's hard to know how to process a feeling if we don't know what it is. So, let's find a name for your uncomfortable feeling.

Sticking with the theme of "no judgment," notice that I'm not saying, "bad feeling." There are no bad feelings. Some feelings feel good, and some feelings feel uncomfortable or displeasing. Just because a feeling is uncomfortable, doesn't make it "bad." Feelings are simply information about something happening inside of you.

You may immediately know what you're feeling. But if it's hard to name your feelings, I recommend keeping a list of feelings close at hand so you can start to identify the feelings that come up for you.

There are countless lists of feelings out in the world. You can use any of them to help you put a name to the feeling. One of my favorite resources for naming feelings is from the book *Ask and It Is Given* by Esther & Jerry Hicks.

The tool they share is the Emotional Guidance System. It's a simple yet clear list of feelings. It helps me to know what I'm feeling and gives me an idea of how I can move toward a feeling that feels better to me.

I also love the book *Atlas of the Heart* by Brené Brown. She goes into well-researched detail about the meaning of over eighty words. It's a powerful read that inspired me so much that I now do a monthly class in the Chaos to Calm Community on "unpacking" the big emotions that come up when we organize.

Here is a list of common feelings that come up when people are organizing their homes:

- Amusement
- Anger
- Annoyance
- Anxiety
- Betrayal
- Boredom
- Calm

- Cognitive Dissonance
- Compassion
- Confusion
- Contentment
- Curiosity
- Defensiveness
- Despair
- Disappointment
- Disconnect
- Discouragement
- Disgust
- Embarrassment
- Excitement
- Fear
- Frustration
- Gratitude
- Grief
- Guilt
- Happiness
- Hate
- Heartbroken
- Hope
- Hopeless
- Humiliation
- Hurt
- Insecurity
- Invisibility
- Jealousy
- Joy
- Loneliness
- Love
- Nostalgia
- Numb
- Overwhelm

- Perfectionism
- Pride
- Reflection
- Regret
- Relief
- Resentment
- Sadness
- Safety
- Scarcity
- Self-Righteousness
- Shame
- Stress
- Surprise
- Tranquility
- Unsafe
- Worry

Your feelings list is a jumping-off point. Sometimes, you may not be able to even put a name to what you're feeling. Remember, it's all about perfect imperfection. Be patient with yourself as you get to know your feelings (and yourself) better.

Knowledge is power. Once you can name what you're feeling, you can set it free.

STEP 4 – PROCESS IT

You've taken the time to explore and name your uncomfortable feeling. Now it's time to set it free. We do this by honoring and acknowledging it. You've got to meet your uncomfortable feeling face to face and see it, exactly as it is.

This step is important because if we don't acknowledge the feeling, it is going to get louder and louder until it has your attention. It will cause so much detriment from trying to be heard that we'll spend more time cleaning up the "collateral damage" than it ever would have taken to face the feeling head-on.

When we process a feeling, we often think we need to re-live the experience or invite it more deeply into our lives. The truth is you don't need to enhance or expand it; just acknowledge that it's here and set it free.

I know the mere thought of inviting a feeling to be present can be terrifying. Maybe you're scared that if you acknowledge a feeling you'll get stuck in it? Or that you'll be trapped in that feeling forever? This is normal and understandable, but the real truth is that if you acknowledge the feeling it will step back, dissipate, and release you. When you don't acknowledge the feeling, it doesn't go away, it simply tries harder to get your attention. Acknowledge it and it will release you.

The other big fear around being present with our uncomfortable feelings is that we don't have time for them. Again, you're trying to get organized. This isn't therapy, you don't want to spend all day feeling your feelings. But feeling feelings is a big part of the organizing process – the part that sets you free. When big feelings show up in our lives, it can feel like we're going to get lost in them and never resurface. It's easy to think, "I don't have time for this." But actually, you don't have time to *not* deal with this. And it will take you far less time than you think. Often, we assume it will take hours to process a feeling, when in fact it only takes seconds. In *My Stroke of Insight*, neuroscientist Jill Bolte-Taylor says that the lifespan of an emotion in the body and brain is ninety seconds. Ninety seconds is how long an emotion will last. You may have several emotions stacked on top of each other, but each will only have a shelf-life of ninety seconds. When you allow yourself to lean fully into feelings for ninety seconds, you invite them to release from your experience.

The journey of processing our feelings looks different for everyone. Some people need to do a deep dig with a therapist; others can talk it out with a friend. Some like to journal, paint, meditate, sing, or go for a run. There's no wrong way to process your feelings. You just have to find a flow that works for you.

Take the time you need to process the feeling that has come up. The more you honor your feelings, the easier it will be to move through these moments of uncomfortable feelings.

Here are a few ideas for how we can process big feelings that arise when we're organizing:

Mindfulness

- Journaling
- Mindfulness Practices
- Breathwork
- Meditation
- Yoga

Get Physical

- Walk
- Run
- Dance

Get Creative

- Sing
- Paint/Draw
- Make Music

- Write a poem
- Bake or cook

Meet Them Head-On

- Intentionally sit with the feeling
- Cry
- Scream
- Punch a pillow
- Twist a towel

"Pen to Paper"

- Journal
- Brainstorm solutions

External Support

- Talk to a trusted person
- Ask someone to sit with you silently
- Ask for a hug or to be held
- Speak to a therapist
- Weighted blanket or compression Blanket
- Bi-lateral stimulation (butterfly hug or bi-lateral stimulation device)

STEP 5 – SHIFT

Now that you've faced the feeling and processed it, let's make sure you can move out of the sticky feeling. Remember, we cannot solve a problem from the energy that created the problem. Meaning, if you want different results, you've got to try new things. We need to move beyond the energy of that uncomfortable emotion and consciously walk a new path.

Processing deep, uncomfortable feelings is powerful. They can be a catalyst for some of the most beneficial and accelerating work we do. But we want to make sure you don't stay stuck in the pain cycle of the uncomfortable feeling. It's important to tune in to what you actually want to experience before you take action again. To do this:

- Ask yourself: "What did that uncomfortable feeling make me realize I want to feel or experience instead?"
- Once you know what that is, take a moment to feel that feeling inside of yourself.
- Visualize yourself experiencing that reality now.
- Notice or look for three ways that what you want is already present in your life.

What if you can't shift away from the uncomfortable feeling? We all get stuck from time to time. That's normal. What's vital is that once you finish processing your uncomfortable feelings (or even just simply holding space for them), you start to move in the direction you want to go. If it feels like too big of a jump to get in touch with a feeling that feels better, you may need a bit more time to process the uncomfortable feeling. Or you may need to reach for a closer feeling. For example, instead of moving from rage to joy, try moving from rage to irritation or annoyance. Look for a smaller jump and always honor what's true for you.

Once you learn to be present with what you want to feel (thanks to experiencing what you didn't like), then you can start to use those feelings as a starting point for taking more mindful, more powerful, more meaningful action. One action taken from an inspired place is more valuable and effective than a hundred taken mindlessly. Don't let hustle culture bully you into thinking that more is better. Sometimes more is just more. Choose quality over quantity.

Doing this will shift you. It will move you in the direction you want to go. This will get you out of the challenging feeling and move you to a more open and expansive place. From this space of knowing what you want to experience, you are ready to start taking action again.

STEP 6 - MOVE FORWARD

Once you're feeling a bit lighter and tapped into a feel-good feeling that you want to experience, continue on with your organizing project.

This step is vital.

Doing this will help you mentally close the loop on your uncomfortable feeling and inspire you to move in the direction you want to go. This is a vital step in rewiring your mind around organization.

In the past, we would let the feelings take us over and derail us. This practice sends a message to your brain that you can move through your challenging feelings and trust yourself to persevere. It affirms your resilience.

The experience of organizing after you process uncomfortable feelings is a powerful practice. It shows you that you can face hard things and keep going. And not only keep going but make beautiful strides too.

Your brain doesn't know the difference between the dopamine hit of winning the slots in Vegas from you creating categories in your pantry or emptying a drawer. It is going to celebrate and say, "Yes, let's keep doing this!" so the best thing you can do is to keep moving forward with your project after you've processed those uncomfortable feelings.

I know that after you've processed some of your uncomfortable feelings, you may feel depleted and want or need a break. Always honor what you need and take care of yourself. However, it's vital that you take even one small step on your organizing project again (even if it only lasts thirty seconds or five minutes) before taking a break.

If you don't have the energy to do a lot more work after you've processed your feelings, even taking one small action will help your brain to close the loop and dial back into feeling grounded again.

RECAP

Let's recap the six steps for managing big, uncomfortable feelings that pop up when you're organizing:

1. Notice something's up
2. Explore it with curiosity
3. Name it
4. Process the feeling
5. Shift
6. Move forward

These simple steps will guide you as you navigate big feelings while organizing. Be gentle with yourself. This is a practice. The more you move through these steps, the more you will learn what works for you, and the easier it will get. Feelings will stop being so scary to face, and you'll move through them with ease during your organizing projects. Plus, you'll find that clutter will build up less because your emotions won't be using clutter to hide or draw attention to painful objects. This is a powerful skill that will benefit every area of your life.

TURNING INSIGHT INTO ACTION

Instead of allowing the big feelings that bubble up to derail you, let's prepare for them. Take time to print out or save the list of feelings that come up when we're organizing (you can get a printable pdf at http://www.starhansen.com/feelings. Having this list accessible as you organize, allows you to be ready to shine a light on any feelings that come up for you. It's time to stop abandoning yourself when big feelings arise and start to get curious and supportive instead.

Next, create a strategy for processing uncomfortable feelings that work for you. I recommend choosing five or more strategies that work best for you. Use the list in this chapter for inspiration. This will make sure that you're ready to face the big feelings that arise as you organize *before* the big feelings take over and shut you down.

7

USE CLUTTER TO UNBLOCK
EVERY AREA OF YOUR LIFE

As I swung open James's bedroom door, I hit a wall. A giant pile of boxes lined the side of the bed, making it impossible to access the partner side of the bed. One side of the room was perfectly organized. Books stacked neatly to be read, alarm clock set at the accurate time, water glass ready for the middle of the night hydration. But the other side was like a land forgotten in time. Half the bed was covered with books, paperwork, electronics, and candy wrappers. He looked down at the non-cluttered walkway leading to his side of the bed and avoided eye contact as we spoke. James's romantic world and self-care were super out of balance and crying for help.

Your spaces give you away. I can walk into your house and tell with a glance what areas of your life are thriving and which are in desperate need of a tune-up. It's not because I have some magical sixth sense, but because I know how to read a room. I know this may limit my dinner invitations but sharing this tool with you is a total life-changer. This power has helped me walk countless people back from feeling out of control in their lives to a place of feeling empowered and at peace with their life. I want to teach you to do the same.

When I walked into Lydia's living room it was clear that she was dying to switch careers. When Jade showed me her dining room, I knew she was hungry for community connection. When Viv and Brandon showed me their bedroom, I instantly saw who wore the pants in the family, and who was feeling second fiddle and building resentment by the hour. The ability to look at the areas of our home and discern if we are out of balance in our life is a superpower. Most people think that the location of their clutter doesn't matter. And yet it speaks volumes to your priorities, as well as challenges.

READ THE ROOM

Think about a room in your home – the one that feels like the hottest of messes, the one you can never get a handle on. Is the clutter here holding you back in specific areas of your life? Now I want you to think about an area of your home that is always dialed in and functional. Your whole world could be falling down, but you will always make sure that this one space is in working order, even if you're the only one who knows what that order is. Does this space help you thrive in specific areas of your life?

Please know – if you can't think of a space that feels functional and dialed in, don't lose heart. It's there, I promise. Just because you can't see it yourself, doesn't mean it's not there. Clutter has a way of skewing our vision. As I've said before, I've never met a disorganized person. You just may be out of touch with the organization in your life. But whether you can see it in this moment or not, it's there.

I've seen it time and time again. We always have at least

one area in our lives and homes that we will fight to protect at all costs. Whether that be our kid's nutrition, our own financial world, or washing our face before bed.

There's something that matters deeply to you and that you make happen no matter what. We've all got it. Our spaces throw a spotlight on what we value, and where we're suffering.

We all have areas in our lives that we struggle with from time to time. Maybe you're going through something, or that part of your life just isn't a priority right now. But sometimes, areas of our lives are really suffering on a chronic level. And our physical clutter can help us determine what parts of our lives need attention most. The rooms of your home hold the key for unblocking the areas of your life.

WAIT, DID I JUST RE-DISCOVER FENG SHUI?

In the Ancient Chinese tradition of feng shui, energy forces of the home are used to help people achieve harmony and balance between people and their environments. Other than taking a one-day feng shui workshop at the local community college two decades ago when I first started my organizing business, I never really studied feng shui. But the more I worked in people's homes, the more I saw parallels between people's cluttered rooms and the struggles they experienced in different areas of their lives. I saw that rooms that were overflowing with clutter became like a spotlight for what parts of their lives were out of balance. I could feel that there was something much deeper going on in people's cluttered rooms.

In some feng shui practices, a Bagua map is used to detail out where certain areas of life are awakened in the home. I love the practice of infusing a home with specific energy based on the home itself. But what I really started to find was that people demonstrate a lot through their spaces. So, I have a slightly different view of the meaning of rooms. Don't get me wrong, I do love feng shui. But unlike feng shui, where the house dictates the energy, I look at the function of the room and your personal experience to dictate the energy.

Every room in your home aligns with an area of your life. The meaning that YOU assign to the rooms. You, your life, priorities, and family determine the meaning of the rooms. And you can determine what a room means by which areas of your life are active for you in those spaces. We'll talk about the meaning of the clutter in the next chapter, for now we're just going to explore the meaning of the rooms.

How you use the rooms, what your values are, and what the rooms symbolize to you say a lot about why clutter builds up in some places and is non-existent in others.

CURIOSITY VERSUS JUDGMENT

Now, to be able to read your rooms, it's vital that you step away from judgment and self-criticism. I know that it's hard to look at your rooms without judgment. Part of you thinks that if you don't judge yourself for your rooms that they will get worse. Being mean to yourself about clutter can be a defense mechanism trying to keep you from letting clutter get out of control. I understand that. But I promise you that judging yourself is on par with bullying. It only leads to pain and dysfunction. In order to transcend the clutter, you've got to move away from judgment and into the world of curiosity, where you look with fresh, open eyes hoping to gather evidence like a scientist. Not looking with an end in mind but just trying to see what is.

From that beautiful world of neutrality, we can start to see the patterns in your spaces. I can see the patterns so easily when I walk into your home because I'm not attached to anything. Sometimes clutter is due to a lack of space, or not having time to put things away. But many times, it's more than that. What we're looking for is not random clutter, but recurring clutter. Clutter that shows up, no matter how many times you try to get rid of it. This is the clutter that has something to say.

Because I have no investment in what I discover, I can see the whole story hiding in your stuff. I have no fear, judgment, or shame about your stuff. I'm just looking at the data. And that's what I want for you. The ability to look at your stuff, separate yourself from what you see (as much as you can, I know this is tricky), and be open to what the rooms are trying to show you.

EXPLORING YOUR WORLD

First things first, we need to get clear about what I mean by Areas of Your Life. These are the main categories of your life. Ways you spend time, things you value, who you are. These are the many facets that make us humans unique and interesting. They exist outside of the world of survival and highlight the ways we use our human resources (time, mental bandwidth, money, thoughts) to spend our lives. Take a peek at the areas of life that humans have the joy of experiencing:

Areas of Life

Spirituality

- Connection to something greater
- Purpose/soul's calling
- Service

Environment

- Sanctuary
- Relationship to the world
- Travel

Relationships

- Intimate relationships
- Sexuality
- Family, friends and community
- Pets

Wellness

- Nourishment
- Fitness
- Rest
- Mental health

Personal Growth

- Relationship with self
- Self-actualization
- Intellectual pursuit
- Emotional intelligence

Play

- Hobbies
- Creativity
- Leisure
- Adventure

Abundance

- Occupation
- Money
- Natural resources (planet)
- Gratitude

It's important for us to start to see the patterns in your life. Take a moment to list out the top three areas of your life that you value most. On a scale of one to five (one is low, five is high) how are those areas of your life going at the moment? Are you living your life according to these values? How does it feel to see how life lines up with your values?

Now let's take this insight to your rooms. I want you to think about the rooms where activities related to your three most valued areas of your life take place or feel most present. You will know these areas of your home because that's where you either do the activities connected with that area of your life, or that's where the objects (or people) connected to that area of your life gather. For example, if you have a lot of paperwork, bills, and work items in your kitchen, that may be your center of abundance more so than your official office back in the guest room. If you spend the most time with your family in the living room, that may be the center of relationships for you. Allow the stuff, spaces, and time you spend show you where the rooms are most active. The lists I share in this chapter are simply a jumping-off point for you to start exploring what's true for you.

As you think about the rooms connected to your three most valued areas of your life, ask yourself the following questions. How do those rooms feel to you? Alive, thriving, stagnant, overwhelming? Just notice. There's no action you need to take right now except to just think about this and see what's there.

Now I want you to think of the three areas of your life that you're struggling most with right now. Which rooms connect most with those areas of your life? How do those rooms feel to you at the moment? Powerful, suffering, joyful, strained? Again, try to stay neutral and just see what is there. This can be a powerful exercise of insight for you.

ROOM MEANINGS

We're going to dig into the meaning of the rooms now. Every room has its own unique purposes and symbolism. Now, you can match the areas of your life with the rooms themselves, but that tends to be a bit too generic and doesn't give us enough insight. Plus, there are some room meanings that are a bit more nuanced.

Below, you'll find a list of rooms and what meaning I have found them to have in nearly two decades of working with people. Now this isn't a one size fits all solution. These are things that I have seen rooms mean over the years, but I want (as always) for you to trust your inner organizing genius and determine for yourself what the rooms mean for you. Each room can have multiple meanings and those meanings can be quite specific, based on how you use the rooms and your own unique interests and values. Take a peek at the meaning of rooms and see what resonates most for you.

Meaning of Rooms

Bathroom

- Releasing toxins
- Emotional truth
- Communication
- Self-expression

Bedroom

- Your identity (for yourself)
- Relationship with yourself
- Self-care
- Rest
- Romance
- Partnership
- Sexuality
- Pleasure

Clothing Closet

- Identity (for the outside world)
- Identity (for yourself)
- Image
- Body image
- Creative expression

Dining Room

- Community
- Time shared with loved ones
- The "airs" we put on
- Social expectations

Entryway

- Connection to the outside world
- Boundaries
- Coming home to yourself
- Launching pad
- Landing pad

Kitchen

- Love
- Nourishment
- Self-care
- Communication

Laundry Room

- Support
- Emotional truth
- Image (from clothing closet items that may overflow here)
- Comfort (from linen closet items that may overflow here)

Linen Closet

- Comfort

- Support
- Readiness
- Guests

Living Room

- Community
- Joy and fun
- Leisure

Office

- Money
- Abundance
- Purpose
- Time

Storage Spaces

- Past
- Future
- Subconscious beliefs
- Unprocessed events
- Overflow from other rooms

What was it like to explore the meanings of rooms? Did anything jump out at you? Did you find yourself agreeing, struggling, uncertain, getting angry, feeling overwhelmed, or feeling relieved? All reactions make perfect sense. We're getting close to seeing what's happening in your stuff. This is so important because the rooms tell us the area of your life that is either healthy or experiencing challenges. The clutter will start to illuminate the patterns that are keeping you stuck. As you learn to decode your rooms and the clutter, you'll start to see deep truths that have the capacity to set you free from clutter and its challenges.

TURNING INSIGHT INTO ACTION

As you reflect on the meaning of your rooms, here are a few good questions to help you explore what's happening in the rooms of your home. What we're doing is exploring what insights the room has for you. Look at only one room at a time; you can even break rooms down into smaller sections or zones if that's easier.

Room Questions

- What are the practical purposes of this room?
- What area of your life does this room symbolize?
- When did the clutter start in this room?
- Did any major events happen around that time?
- Who is connected to this room?
- What activities feel connected to this room?
- Did any significant events or memories happen here?
- How do you feel in this room?

Great work starting to uncover the meaning of your rooms! The spaces of your home are alive and act as a microcosm of your life. This plays a key role in using your clutter genius to set you free. If possible, allow yourself to explore the rooms in a playful way – much like a kid explores their imagination. Trust you intuition to guide you and know that there's nothing you will discover that will destroy you. Exploration is an important part of you using your clutter to come home to yourself.

8

DISCOVER THE MESSAGE IN YOUR MESS

What do a pile of college catalogs, boxes of unpacked kitchen appliances, and overflowing bathroom drawers of lipstick have in common? They're all telling a very specific tale about someone's life. There is no accident when it comes to the types of items we surround ourselves with. We don't accidentally come across twenty-five shades of red lipstick, twenty weeks of unopened mail, or 137 pairs of designer jeans. These are choices we make based on some kind of subconscious drive within us. These stacks of papers, overflowing drawers of clothing and unpacked boxes in the garage are all telling a specific story. And no, that's not a scary story blaming you for all that's wrong in your life.

These are external patterns of something happening inside of you. And if we look at the items that make up the clutter around you, we can start to shape the story of you. And most importantly, your clutter highlights what you need in order to thrive, release the clutter, and be fulfilled in a way you've never experienced before. There's a message in your mess and it's waiting for you to see it.

CLUTTER REVEALS PATTERNS IN YOUR LIFE

People are so quick to judge their clutter. To see it as a bothersome flaw that needs to be rooted out and eliminated. But then they're surprised when it continues to return over and over again. If we can stop trying to constantly purge, and instead lean in and get curious about what's really happening in the clutter, only then can we actually eliminate the clutter for good.

Let me start by saying that this can be a scary thing to do. We have so many negative feelings about ourselves, and our lives tied up in our clutter. You may need to re-read Chapter 5 (Why Organizing Drains Your Energy) a few times before this isn't excruciatingly scary to consider. It's safe to let go of those fears for now. Indulging in those fears will not make this easier for you, it only serves to distract you from what's really happening here.

WHAT IS CLUTTER?

Society at large will say that clutter is disorganized stuff. Or perhaps an untidy state, or a crowded, chaotic, disordered collection of stuff. Maybe you think of it as stuff you don't need. At its most basic sense, clutter is simply a collection of personal property. Objects. Stuff. Possessions. Things. That's all. The value, emotions, and shame are assigned by us.

If you have a room filled with unopened mail, you may feel a lot of anxiety and fear. But if I tell you that room of unopened mail is filled with birthday cards stuffed with cash, you may feel excited and overjoyed. It's the same stuff, but the value assigned is different. Know that the power of the clutter is assigned by *you*. The value might be determined by something you feel about this moment of your life, or it might have been based on beliefs handed to you early in life that you're still connecting to. The beauty of you being the originator of clutter's value and energy is that you can change it at any time. You get to choose whether your clutter has the power to break you or elevate you. My hope is that together, we can use it to elevate you.

To me, clutter is beautiful. It's proof of a life well lived. It shows that you have interests, hobbies, loved ones, passions, adventures…. It tells the story of your life. And that's a beautiful and powerful thing. It's time to change the narrative around clutter and start to see it as a friend.

DOES YOUR CLUTTER HAVE A PATTERN?

We are creatures of habit. And so often we're living in this unconscious state where we do things without thinking about them. Or, sometimes, we do things to avoid thinking about something else entirely. So, what happens with clutter is that it reveals a pattern unique to you. This clutter pattern is serving you in some way. Sometimes we use our clutter to help us remember to do something important. Other times we use it as a hint to tell someone what we need. Maybe we use it to help us hide, or we might use it to solidify painful lessons we don't want to forget.

Jeremy experienced a home invasion last year. They broke into his house and stole electronics as well as cash, checks, jewelry, and other valuables. When we met, he was really struggling with the clutter in his office. The rest of the house was organized and functional, but he had this huge resistance to getting rid of paperwork in the office. He would get agitated when things were organized, and then he would backslide all over again. He realized that he was terrified to get organized because the clutter was helping him hide things from potential burglars. If the office was in a state of chaos, burglars couldn't steal his valuables because they couldn't find them. Until he addressed his need for security, he was unable to let go of the clutter.

Zoe saw a model in a magazine using the most beautiful red lipstick they had ever seen. Somehow, they got it into their mind that if they could find the perfect shade of red lipstick, they would finally feel beautiful, and their life would be magically perfect. Anytime they saw a red lipstick, they would buy it. But none of them were quite right. Each one was a little bit wrong for any number of reasons. So, their bathroom was overflowing with lipstick, trying to help them discover their beauty and create their dream life.

Clutter is telling a specific story. And when you can hear what clutter is trying to tell you, you'll be able to break free from it. Let's explore some ways you can see the message in your mess.

IS CLUTTER TALKING TO YOU?

First things first, we need to know if, in fact, clutter is trying to talk to you. You might be reading this thinking; there's no way clutter is talking to me. Or this might be the balm you've been looking for because you've known for a while now that something big is happening in your clutter. Let's start with knowing if clutter is talking to you. Because if it is, clutter has a message for you. And it's not going to go away until you hear what it has to say. Here are a few ways to know if clutter is trying to talk to you:

How to Know If Clutter Is Talking to You

- Your internal alarm bells go off whenever you're near your clutter.
- You feel terrified or ashamed of people seeing your clutter.
- You think about clutter a lot … like, *a lot,* a lot.
- The idea of getting rid of your clutter scares you or makes you super uncomfortable.
- It's stopping you from starting or finishing something.
- You think that having clutter means something negative about you.
- Clutter feels like a heavy weight, weighing you down.
- There's a pattern to *what* objects you clutter and *where* your clutter is collecting.
- You feel haunted by people or events when you try to handle your clutter.
- It's like Groundhog Day – no matter how many times you get rid of it, it keeps coming back over and over again.

How many of these ring true for you? If you had more than three, chances are good that clutter is trying like crazy to talk to you. What do you do now? Well, it's time to dig a little deeper.

DISCOVER THE ORDER IN YOUR CHAOS

There's nothing random about the recurring clutter in your life. Recurring clutter is clutter that shows up over and over again, no matter what you do. It tends to be made up of similar objects, collected in specific locations. These are the items that continue to build up despite your repeated efforts to get organized. And these items will magically call-in other clutter to help keep it hidden.

The objects that make up the clutter in your life and the way it's building up can help you discover what's keeping it in your life. Only when you see the order in your chaos, can you actually free yourself of it. I know it sounds like I'm anthropomorphizing clutter here but hear me out. I've had years of seeing the deeper meaning buried in people's stuff. Even science says that there is order in chaos. Think of Chaos Theory. It says that chaotic systems often have an underlying order. I've found this to be absolutely true with clutter. Together, we're going to discover the order in your chaos.

There are several markers that will give you insight into your clutter:

- Function
- Origin
- Connection
- Feelings
- Pattern

These elements will invite you to see your clutter in a new way. They won't all apply to you. That's okay. Usually, one of the five contains the answer we're looking for. Look for the one that speaks to you most. Each one has valuable information for you. Think of this process as a clutter inquiry. As we explore each of these elements of your clutter, I want you to ask yourself if it resonates for you. What we're looking for as we explore these different facets of your clutter is what lights up for you. It will feel like an alarm is going off inside of you when we hit the right one.

Sometimes the alarm feels like a deep knowing inside of

you. Other times it may come across as rage, frustration, or annoyance. You may get really tired and want to take a nap (that's resistance trying to keep you safe). You may find yourself flooded with insight, or with a list of actions that you feel drawn to complete. Just notice when that alarm goes off for you.

As we explore the message in your mess, it's important to simplify your view. I don't want you trying to make sense of dozens (or hundreds) of items all at once. I want you to pick one specific type of item and to start to unpack its deeper meaning. For example, if clothes are your recurring clutter, pick the category of clothing that recurs most often, like jeans or scarves. Or if your pantry is overflowing, are baking items taking up the most space, or is it snack foods? Get specific. You want to pick an object that has a history of being recurring clutter in your life and home. Once you've determined the object, let's discover the order in your chaos.

Function

Aubrey was tired of not being able to sit on her couch. Every inch was piled high with pillows. Throw pillows, sleeping pillows of all shapes and sizes, body pillows, pillows that still had tags on them. It was like a home store in her family room! As we decluttered the pillows, she discovered that they were doing two things. First, they were comforting her. Her kids were no longer babies and didn't need her as much. She missed the snuggles and sweetness of their younger years and felt overwhelmed by the complexity of the current teenage years. Secondarily, these pillows gave her something to focus on. They gave her a purpose and offered the promise of a "perfect home" – one that was well decorated, and where everyone loved to spend time together. As long as she was collecting pillows and creating her dream home, she was able to distract herself from her discomfort around her current life – not knowing what she was supposed to do now that her babies were almost grown, and feeling dissatisfied with being the invisible, unappreciated home caretaker. The minute we got rid of the pillows it was like we pulled the scab off of a gaping wound. The pillows were there to comfort her both physically and emotionally, as well as give her purpose. Without them, she couldn't ignore the truth ringing inside of her.

Function is all about practicality. Function gives us important information about what the clutter may be helping us achieve in our lives. There are two questions you want to ask yourself here. The first question is: what does this object do? As in, what is its purpose in the most basic sense? It's a simple question but it opens the door to seeing deeper patterns. In the case of Aubrey's pillows, pillows support us, make us feel comfortable, make a space look beautiful, allow us to express our creativity through our spaces. That's just what pillows do in the most practical sense. Once we see that, we can start to consider if there's a deeper purpose in the object doing that for us in our lives.

The second question you want to ask is: what is this object doing for me? This is where we leave the realm of basic function and look at our behavior with the object. We look at what we're trying to do with the item. In Aubrey's case, she was trying to use the pillows to bring her family together again for close, bonding time they could no longer squeeze into their busy days. Plus, she was using it to feel purposeful in her life. She spent time trying to create the perfect home when she felt like she was lost and uncertain about her life. Both types of functionalities were active with Aubrey's pillows, and it gave us great insight into what she needed beyond the clutter.

Origin

Next, let's look at the origin of the item. When did this pattern of clutter begin? Has it been like this since you were a child? Or did this pattern really take off after a specific incident in your life? Organizing is like an archeological dig. There's always information in the clutter. We're looking for insight as to why and when the clutter pattern may have begun.

Myla doesn't remember being cluttered when she was younger. She may not have been perfectly organized, but she managed to balance a career, family, and home without any major incident. And then her husband died unexpectedly. When he died, the world spun out of control, and she did what she could to just move forward. Years later, she was buried in clutter and felt overwhelmed by every scrap of paper. When we started to explore when the clutter began, it was clear that it really started when her husband passed. There were practical things that caused the clutter (like the fact that he managed the family bills, and she didn't even know their online banking passwords or account information), plus the deep grief that she felt about living without him. Understanding when the clutter began helps highlight the practical and emotional support that is needed to move beyond the chaos.

Connection

Sung loved her Korean heritage. Even though she had only been there once on vacation, she felt drawn to all things Korean. Her guest room was filled with embroidered pillows, traditional Hanbok dresses from her aunties, paper fans, family photographs, and boxes of glazed ceramic dishes. She didn't have room to display it all, but it made her happy to collect and just know she had it. It made her feel connected to her family and her heritage.

Who, what, or when does this clutter make you feel connected to? Often, we use clutter as a connector, keeping us attached to people we love, times in our lives that brought us joy, or events that we remember fondly. Sometimes, we may even use clutter to keep us connected to negative things as well. I've seen people use physical objects to remind them of bad things that happened, so they don't ever experience it again. It's like a warning to themselves to do things differently.

Getting clear about what we're trying to stay connected to, allows us to choose intentional ways to include those people, places, or times in our lives, without needing to collect stuff. Instead of having a room full of collected items that feel chaotic, what if you made a mindful choice to decorate a whole room dedicated to this pursuit? I had an amazing client once who had one of the best experiences of her life at a Beatles concert, and later decorated her office with all things Beatles. She was able to enjoy her memorabilia, and her office felt so much more fun for her to work in, too.

Feelings

Every time Lexi saw a piece of jewelry, she felt a surge of energy and joy. She found herself collecting gorgeous pieces of antique costume jewelry online and anywhere she traveled. She had amazing taste and found the most incredible pieces. But soon her house was overflowing with jewelry. The thing that brought her joy, suddenly made her feel suffocated. It wasn't until she decided to turn her jewelry collection into a decorative display that she was able to truly enjoy the jewelry in her life.

What feelings do you feel about an item that keeps piling up in your home? Knowing how you feel about certain items will help you understand what might be happening for you with your clutter. If you feel joy when you see an item, it may cause you to want to see it by leaving it out or collecting more. If you feel anxious, annoyed, or ashamed about an item, it may cause you to want to bury that item under lots of other stuff to keep it hidden. How you feel about an item is an important clue when it comes to your clutter. It will give you guidance as to how you might be behaving with it.

Pattern

Carmen was always starting new projects without finishing the last ones. She had a hunger for life and an effervescent creativity that was contagious. But the habit of starting new projects without finishing the old ones was really tripping her up – literally! When we started to work together, she had recently tripped over a pile of clutter (an unfinished project she lost interest in) and broke her foot. She needed to get organized because the clutter was literally hurting her. As we explored the type of clutter that was in her home, a pattern emerged. She had stacks along the floor of almost every room in her house – both blocking her and tripping her. The pattern of how her stuff showed up was clear. Her clutter was mostly unfinished projects. And these unfinished projects were tripping her up and blocking her from getting anything done. Once we knew what was going on, we started to explore ideas for how she could manage projects she lost interest in. For some of them, she had to commit to not finishing them and give them away or toss them. For others, she made the decision she wanted to finish them, gave herself a deadline, and scheduled time with friends to do Body Doubling sessions where they got together to work on their own individual projects in order to help aid completion, focus, and accountability.

Your clutter is as unique as you are. It has its own pattern, shape, and flow. Believe it or not, there's powerful insight in whether you have things shoved into empty paper garbage bags, piled on every surface, stashed in your "room of doom", or covering every inch of the floor in your office. Maybe you've got "flat-space-itis" (the inability to not pile stuff onto the flat surfaces of your home). Maybe you are a piler. Maybe you're a shover. There's a pattern to your clutter and understanding what it is will help you transform your clutter once and for all.

The pattern of your stuff contains many clues for what clutter is doing in your life. The pattern often points to the message directly. Notice what you say when you get frustrated by your stuff. "Ugh, I feel so blocked in here!" "I'm buried in paperwork." Just as Carmen's clutter was "tripping" her up, your clutter may be doing the same for you. Look to the pattern of your clutter for clues as to what your clutter may be doing to or for you.

Look around. Do you notice any patterns when it comes to how your stuff shows up in the spaces of your home? Is every square inch of your floor covered? Or do you like to pile things high on counters? Do you see no visible clutter in your rooms, but know you'll be smothered by an avalanche of stuff if you open your closet? You might have bursts of clutter in specific areas of your home. Or it might look like an earthquake hit and your home is reeling from the aftermath. Is your clutter blocking you in any way, or restricting you? Maybe you can't enter a room because clutter is blocking access. Or certain functions or actions within the room are restricted. Is it hard to see here? Hard to move? Is it uninviting to anyone specifically?

Don't try to jump into action from this insight. I just want you to start to be aware of what you see. Sometimes, as you start to see the pattern of your clutter, you will get insight as to what you need to do next. That's what we're looking for – an inner call to action that stems from your innate Organizing Genius. I could tell you a million possible things you could do, but you are the only person who can hear what your clutter is telling you and who knows the right action for you. My job is to awaken your ability to hear your Organizing Genius so you can start taking the right action for *you*.

IS CLUTTER HIDING SOMETHING?

One of the most common patterns I see in clutter is hiding. Life brings us painful experiences, and clutter can remind us of those experiences. Often it feels overwhelming to have to confront that pain day after day, so we bury it in our clutter.

I was helping to move Tony to assisted living. His office was buried in stacks of paper and office supplies. As I dove into the paperwork, I discovered a consistent pattern – they all had the same timeline. The piles of clutter here all started in 2011. I asked him, "What happened in 2011?" That's the year my best friend died. Tony's clutter was helping him bury his pain, and also highlighted the challenges of trying to "get back to life" while we're in a deep state of grief after someone we love passes away.

When we have an object that reminds us of a wound we've sustained, our psyche may try to help by burying it under layers of clutter. Most of our clutter is actually pretty neutral. But the items that feel like little nuggets of pain can cause the other clutter in our life to feel excruciating because they're working to hide the painful items. This is one of the reasons de-cluttering can feel so difficult. For example, maybe you're organizing and folding t-shirts. But if one of those t-shirts belonged to your now deceased mother or was something you wore at the time of a sexual assault, a simple task like folding can feel complex or overwhelming. In that case, the item of clothing can ignite a deep, painful wound for you. The task of folding and organizing shirts becomes much more difficult when there's a triggering item mixed in. Often it feels safer to have the painful item buried in clutter where it can't be seen or felt.

It's important to seek out the nuggets of pain and either handle them or tuck them away in a safe (and well-labeled) place until you're ready to handle them.

I have a box of VHS tapes sitting in my garage. I'm not ready to let them go but I also can't face them. I remember looking at one of the tapes when I was in a fiery organizing mood – ready to tackle the past and organize it all. The first video I played flashed to a clip of me and my sister at our childhood home. She wanted to play with me, and I was annoyed and bothered that my little sister was trying to be included. I was your typical, ever-irritated big sister, wanting my own autonomy and tired of my little sister tagging along everywhere I went. But because of my sister's suicide, watching that tape ripped me in half. It triggered all my trauma around her death – the way I blamed myself, my countless regrets with her, my inability to face life without her. I shut the VHS player off and put the tape away. I just couldn't face it yet. I still can't, to be honest. Just seeing one of those tapes can send me into a whirlwind of grief and shame.

I now have those tapes boxed, labeled, and stored in the garage so they can't sneak up on me and emotionally stab me in unexpected moments. I'm not ready to face them yet, but I know one day I will be able to. It doesn't "spark joy" but it is a path I need to walk, and one day I will. Or I won't, and that's okay. But, in the meantime, it won't clutter my home, daily life, and emotional world anymore.

NOT ALL CLUTTER IS SCARY

The general idea of clutter can be overwhelming. Big boxes stuffed to the brim with who knows what. Grocery bags leaning against the wall from hurried clean-up efforts when guests arrived unannounced. Does that overflowing box of stuff contain bills you never paid or love letters from high school? Looking at our clutter from a distance can feel terrifying and even paralyzing.

Priya was organizing her basement when she came across a stack of unopened cardboard boxes from who knows when. The minute she saw them, her stomach turned. A few had water damage, some were crushed under the weight of each other. None of them looked familiar to her. She wanted to do anything but open them. Yet, they were the last remaining things that needed to be handled in order to complete her basement organizing project. So, with great dread, she pulled down the top box and started to go through it. As she unpacked it, a huge smile came across her face. It was packed with her childhood schoolwork. Something about the old-style paper and seeing her familiar childhood handwriting, warmed her heart. This collection of paper felt calming, nostalgic, and fun. She took a few pages upstairs and showed her kids. They all gushed over the memories for a while, then Priya went back downstairs, selected a few pages to add to her memory box, and threw the rest away. What started out as an annoying, terrifying task ended up being a heartwarming, joyful exploration of her past. The remaining boxes no longer felt daunting, and she charged forward, excited to see what else she might discover.

The details of clutter can be quite fun. Not always, but often, there are treasures hiding in our clutter that can be enjoyable to explore. It can be interesting, fun, and hold a lot of beauty. The macro is overwhelming, but the micro of clutter can be exciting.

As you start to reimagine clutter's purpose in your life, I want you to consider the layers of clutter. It's important to be able to explore what might be happening in your clutter, but it's also just as important to be in touch with the practical purpose and use of the item. For example, when Zoe was collecting lipstick, we needed to name that lipstick's practical purpose which was to make Zoe feel beautiful. That insight is so basic but also gets overlooked sometimes. I recommend you look at specific types of objects (i.e., unopened mail, jeans, towels, etc.) instead of seeing your clutter as a giant mass of random stuff. Freedom is in the details. The more dialed in, the better. Remember, we're trying to explore patterns in the chaos.

TURNING INSIGHT INTO ACTION

I know it can feel like a lot to start to explore the clutter in your life from this new perspective. Try not to tackle everything all at once (a common mistake in organizing). Instead, I want you to pick just one object that you struggle with and see if you can start to see a theme laced in there. For example, instead of "kitchen counter paperwork," look for a theme. Is it unopened medical bills? Or kids' artwork? What is the common theme here? Use the following questions to start to see the insights that might be buried in your clutter:

Clutter Questions

- What does this object do?
- What is this object doing for me?
- When did this pattern of clutter begin?
- Who, what, or when does this clutter make me feel connected to?
- How do you feel about this item?
- What is the pattern of this clutter? (Blocking, tripping, suffocating, etc.)
- If this item could speak, what would it say?
- How might this object be helping you?
- What do things give you that people don't?

Starting to look at the details of your clutter can be a game-changer. When we see all clutter as simply clutter, we miss out on the details that can help us dig ourselves out of the chaos. Seeing the truth buried in your clutter is what sets you free. Now that you've started to see the deeper layers of your clutter, it's time to go a little deeper and discover how your clutter might actually be helping you – and how you can turn that insight into a life without clutter.

9

DECODING HOW CLUTTER IS ACTUALLY HELPING YOU

I know you don't want clutter in your life anymore. But what if you need clutter? What if clutter is meeting your needs in a way that you never realized?

When I started working with Val, her bedroom would just not stay clean and organized. We would spend a full day getting everything dialed in, systems created, pared down to the essentials, feeling happy and great, but then within a few weeks, the clutter would pile back up again. After doing this together for a few months, I asked Val how her clutter might be helping her. She thought about it for a while and said, "When my room's a mess, my parents can't come in here. I feel like I can actually have my privacy." She was using her clutter to create privacy for herself.

I said, "What if you continued to use clutter to keep your parents out and protect your privacy, but you stopped drowning yourself in clutter? What if you allow yourself to fill the first three feet of your room with clutter, but the rest of it needs to stay organized and clear for you? You can keep your "wall of protection" but give yourself a safe space to be happy and fulfilled in your life – without the clutter covering every surface. There's no need for clutter to hurt you – let it do what you need it to do."

As she leaned into the idea that clutter was helping her create privacy, she started getting her needs met in more direct ways and she stopped needing her clutter. Her room stayed organized, including the wall of clutter we had created in the first three feet of her room. There was something about recognizing that clutter was helping her get her needs met that allowed her to find alternatives to meeting her own needs. Clutter helped give her a safe hiding space in her home – autonomy from her family. It also allowed her to recognize that she needed to create safe "hiding" spaces for items that felt vulnerable to her, like her journal and the books she was reading. Asking her parents to not come in when she needed privacy didn't seem so hard to ask for now that she knew what was really going on. When Val recognized how she was using clutter to get her needs met, she was able to meet those needs without the chaos, and the clutter stopped showing up.

CLUTTER SATISFIES YOUR NEEDS

If a pattern of recurring clutter exists in your life, chances are pretty good that it's serving you in some way. Clutter is meeting a need. Now I know this sounds crazy but stay with me for a minute.

Sienna's bedroom was overflowing with towels, bathrobes, and cozy clothes. Half her room's footprint was devoted to this cozy clutter. Most of the items had come from the bathroom. The bathroom, as you remember from Chapter 7, is the space for releasing emotions. It's where we go to release toxins, dirt, and other ickiness from our bodies. Once we release these toxins, we are immediately comforted with some sort of cozy thing. A towel after a shower, a tissue for our nose, T.P. for our – well, you get the idea. So, why was Sienna collecting soothing, cozy things in her bedroom, the center of partnership and self-care? Well, she was married to a toxic man who she wasn't able to leave (no judgment, not everyone can make large sweeping changes in their lives, sometimes we need to make the best of a challenging situation). Because she felt like she was constantly inundated with his toxic energy, she felt the need to be comforted and create a safe space within the chaos of the household and her relationship. The towels, robes, and cozy clothes gave her that comforting, safe space.

As we explored this need for comfort more deeply, we started to think about what kind of things might provide her comfort from the toxicity, without the clutter. I asked her to make a list of ten things that might do the trick. A recurring theme appeared – a pet. She was happiest when she had a pet. If she had a dog, she would feel comforted and loved. Plus, she would have something to give her attention to, as well as a safe excuse to leave the house for a walk when things got to be too much at home. She found a solution that met her actual need, while supporting her unique situation. With her need for comfort being met, the pile of cozy clutter disappeared – and it didn't feel hard or painful. She was making space for her new friend and the clutter was no longer needed.

When you meet the actual need your clutter has been providing in a non-clutter way, you'll be able to release the clutter more easily. Because it's no longer needed, the clutter can feel less painful or complicated to manage. Sometimes it even feels like it just effortlessly falls away. And that's what I want for you.

I know it can seem like a big stretch to think that your clutter is meeting some deeper need, but if you have recurring clutter in specific locations, that is exactly what it's doing. You are a strong, smart, powerful being. You've done a lot of hard things in your life. And, as much as clutter can be challenging, you are totally capable of getting a handle on it. If you haven't been able to do so yet, usually that's because it's filling some greater need. My job is to help you discover what that is.

LOOKING AT CLUTTER WITH NEW EYES

Our knee-jerk reaction is to classify clutter as bad, and that we are bad for having it. But, what if, instead of doing the same old thing, you flipped the narrative. What if, instead of shoving the clutter back in its box, putting it in the trash, or donating it, you first took a moment to say hello and see how it might be trying to help you? The truth is that if clutter is talking to you, it has a message for you. In some way, it's trying to help you. This is clutter wisdom – hearing the message that clutter is trying to share with you. Clutter possesses a deep insight into your personal truths. Each time you set something down on your kitchen counter, purchase another pair of jeans, or shove those towels back in the closet, part of you is trying to achieve something.

I understand that the concept of helpful clutter is a strange one. It can feel completely counterintuitive. It can be so strange to think of clutter being a helpful friend, and yet, that's exactly what it's doing.

It's easy to feel like clutter is all bad. It's often loaded with stuff that feels bad, but it's also full of lots of wonderful things too. When we talk about clutter meeting a need, there are many wonderful things it is trying to do, and some not so nice ones. I know it may seem counterintuitive, but when clutter is doing something not so nice, it still thinks it's helping. It's just a little misguided. Much like in Chapter 6 when we talked about how looking for what's wrong in ourselves is often a defense mechanism (trying to make us be a better version of ourselves), many times these cluttered items are trying to do the same. They're attempting to help, even if it is done in a not so good-feeling way.

So, how might clutter be trying to help you? There are countless ways, but I find that most fall under eight simple categories of attempted helpful behaviors:

Empower

First and foremost, clutter is amazing at empowering us. An accumulation of stuff allows us to feel abundant or like our needs are met. I know that many people who lived through the great depression needed to experience the sensation of their needs being met by having a fully stocked pantry. Many people were raised by parents or grandparents who lived in homes where this was a high value. Being raised by someone who needed to affirm their needs were met affects how we experience waste, let go of things, how we stock our home, etc.

Clutter may hold reminders of wonderful chapters of your life, or things you have accomplished in your life. Seeing those things around you may ignite a sense of pride, importance, or strength. Clutter is also a true proof of life, so you may look at the things around you and remember the wonderful life you've lived and those you've loved. Some people feel most themselves surrounded by stuff. And it can feel uncomfortable to think of living without clutter surrounding them, even if they like the idea of having an organized, minimalist home.

Clutter may empower you to stand up for yourself. It

might give you an excuse to not have people over. Or maybe it allows you to rebel against things you feel like you "should" do, but actually don't want to do, such as host overnight guests or have a party.

Connect

Clutter can be a brilliant connector. Physical objects bond us to people, events, places, and ideas. These items are kept because they bring us happy memories. They remind us of things we want to feel and remember.

Most people have some kind of clutter that never seems to find a home. I call this Lost Clutter. I think one of the most prevalent types of Lost Clutter is sentimental items that remind us of people, places, or events we cherish. Often these items don't have a home and just float aimlessly around the house. We want to be reminded of them, so we just shuffle them from place to place, wanting to hold them close but having no idea where they belong in our lives. (A great habit is to create a Memory Box to store keepsakes that bring you joy so they aren't floating around the house getting lost.)

Clutter can also allow us to feel connected to ourselves. Think of something in your home that has always been there, something that makes you feel at home. For me, this is a little yellow chicken my mom gave me the first time I moved away from home. She told me it was to help me never forget where I come from. After dozens of moves across the country, I still have that chicken. It's the difference between "place of residence" and "my home."

Remind

Oh clutter, you're such a great reminder! The old saying "out of sight, out of mind" describes perfectly why clutter can be so prevalent. We often leave items out that we want to remember to take action on. Clutter is amazing at that.

We also surround ourselves with stuff to remind us of our goals, or to help support us on a path of growth. Think of those little post-its around your house reminding you of a mantra, self-care step, or practitioner you want to hire. Often, we use clutter to help us remember who we're trying to be by leaving a trail of breadcrumbs showing us how to get there.

Communicate

Clutter speaks! And I don't just mean the silent scream of clutter urging you to pay a bill, return something, or telling you that you're lazy for having clutter. I mean clutter speaks for you. So many times, we communicate non-verbally with others through our stuff.

I once had a partner who I felt frustrated with because our experience of what a clean house should look like was very different. I felt like I was doing all the cleaning. I wanted to get support in caring for the house, but he was so busy with work, and he wasn't comfortable with us hiring a housekeeper. After unsuccessfully asking several times for support, I was frustrated, angry and feeling powerless. One morning I got out of bed and thought, well if he doesn't care about the state of the house, then why bother. I left the room that day without making the bed. (Gasp, shock, horror! I'm so wild!) I was trying to "show him" by leaving physical evidence that said, "fine, if you're not going to support me, then I'm not going to give as much." The joke, unfortunately, was on me because he didn't care at all about having the bed made and didn't even notice. But it was good insight for me to see how different our values and needs were. I was trying to talk to him through my stuff because I felt powerless after trying, unsuccessfully, to get my needs met directly.

Clutter can be an extension of our voice. Sometimes it's easier to say it with clutter. It lets us feel like we've exercised our power, without having to be directly confrontational. Maybe we don't feel safe to ask for what we need. Or we aren't comfortable setting a boundary with someone. Or don't know how to name what it is that we truly need.

Nurture

Clutter can be so comforting! The experience of being surrounded with stuff can feel like a warm hug. It can make you feel not so alone in this world. I've had clients tell me that humans feel unsafe to them, but that their clutter is always steady, present, and "there" for them. Many people who grew up in military families experienced instability in their homes. Having to move frequently, "stuff" becomes the one constant. Clutter can feel like a friend when it's one of the only constants in your life.

Protect

Protection is a need that clutter is always happy to fulfill. Sometimes, clutter is there to help protect valuables from being found or stolen. Other times it protects us from others. When I was a kid, we lived on a busy street. The sound of the cars driving by at night would scare me and I had fears of someone sneaking into my bedroom at night.

One day, my sister and I decided we would keep ourselves safe by sleeping in the same bed, and then piling all of our toys and books on her bed (which was under the window) so that if someone snuck into our room through the window, we would hear them coming, trip them, and be able to escape.

Clutter can also be used to help us feel like we're protecting the planet by not being wasteful. It can feel so bad to throw things away, especially when they have served us well. So often people keep things thinking they're going to repair them before giving them away, or that they're going to take the time to find the right "forever home" for their unwanted clutter and furniture. These beautiful intentions build up quickly and frequently lead to feeling overwhelmed and paralyzed by having too much to do in order to declutter.

Hide

The beauty of clutter's chaos is that it gives you amazing places to hide. You can use clutter to bury items that remind you of painful people, events, and chapters of your life that you're not ready to process. It's also great at allowing you to bury painful feelings and avoid dealing with them.

Clutter can help you hide from others, events, work, responsibilities, or deadlines, pretty much anything unwanted. Clutter is a great scapegoat and mechanism for needing to be "busy" or not being able to participate when you don't want to.

Always "needing" to handle your clutter, can give you time for yourself, and can create physical space for yourself away from others. Gerald once told me that he actually liked having a cluttered car because his only time alone all day was on his commute, and the clutter stopped him from giving people a ride home.

Clutter can also help you hide from being seen. Clutter is a great smoke screen that distracts others from seeing our true essence. If they can only see the chaos of our stuff, we can feel safely hidden in the clutter.

Punish

Okay, this one is the hardest one. I mean, how is it helpful to punish ourselves with clutter? It seems like that wouldn't be helpful. But sadly, there are many ways clutter offers us support with punishment. Sometimes, a part of us thinks we need to punish ourselves for certain things in our lives that didn't go the way we wanted them to go. Maybe you've never forgiven yourself for that mistake you made at work years ago, and you want to keep items that remind you of it as a reminder to not make the same mistake again.

Or if you feel like you're responsible for someone getting hurt, a part of you may feel like you deserve to continue to blame yourself and be reminded of the pain so you can "pay your dues." I say a part of you because I know that you know this isn't completely true. But sometimes, we have unresolved challenges inside of us that we are still working on healing. It isn't the full story, but it's part of it.

Maybe you're keeping things because you blame someone else for something and having certain items makes your rage feel justified. In my TEDx talk, I share the story of a couple who left a broken teacup on their counter for over a year because they each blamed the other for it being broken. It's nothing to be ashamed of. We're all working on healing, evolving, and growing from this wild ride called life.

Once you can start to see clutter, not as an enemy, but as a friend who is trying to help you, you can allow yourself to shift your story with clutter. And from that place you can see the real pattern happening under the surface. With that realization, you can unlock yourself from a lifetime of patterns, fears, chaos, and anxiety. Clutter didn't cause those things, but it can help perpetuate it. And that insight will actually help you solve it in a lasting way. As long as you don't address the deeper message in the mess, you'll keep recreating it. And worse, you might actually get organized but pass the message off to another area of your life (like your health, romantic relationships, etc.). The sooner you get the message, the sooner that part of you can heal and then you won't need clutter (or anything else) to help you cope.

You are not your stuff. And yet, your stuff is an expression of you – and chances are it's helping you meet a need.

Where we get challenged is when we have a negative judgment about our clutter. When this is the case, asking ourselves "is clutter helping me?" can be terrifying. Because if I view clutter as shameful and horrible, and/or if other people have judged or attacked me for my clutter, then it wouldn't feel safe to identify with my clutter. If I think clutter is horrible, then I definitely don't want to identify with my clutter. I don't want to be a horrible person. I don't want to think that clutter is speaking on behalf of me because "clutter is bad, and I don't want to be bad. I'm not identifying with that." But doing this stops us from seeing the beautiful Clutter Wisdom that can set us free from the chaos once and for all.

The more you can lean into that friendship with clutter, the more you can start to meet your needs in another, more direct way. The goal is for you to get your actual needs met and then use the energy you've been expending on handling (and / or avoiding) your clutter, to live the life of your dreams. You can redirect those resources to yourself, your loved ones, your career, your hobbies, wherever you want to direct it. It's possible to meet your needs without physical stuff. And when you stop trying to meet your needs with clutter, you get that energy back again. I want to return all of that energy to you.

HOW TO MEET YOUR NEEDS

Let's jump in first and strengthen your foundation by exploring the concept of needs. In our modern world, the idea of having needs is often perceived as being selfish or desperate. But the truth is that all humans have needs. And when we have our needs met, we are much more functional, effective, and capable. When talking about needs, psychologists often reference Maslow's Hierarchy of Needs. This theory explores humankind's essential needs. It covers everything from air, food, shelter, community, confidence, self-actualization, morality, and intimacy. Humans have needs. And the more our basic needs are met, the more capable we are of functioning on higher levels.

It's not bad to have needs, it's an intrinsic part of who we are. And the sooner we realize this, the more we can see that having our needs met will allow us to be better in every area of our lives, and for everyone in our lives. Similar to what we discussed in Chapter 6 about big feelings associated with clutter, when we judge or ignore our needs, the need doesn't go away; it gets louder.

As you allow yourself to be in touch with your needs, you can start to see how these needs are helping you achieve a healthy, thriving life. It's vital to know how to meet our own needs. And when we've been out of touch with our needs for a while, it's easy to be completely overwhelmed when we think about meeting our own needs. For many of us, it's way easier to think about helping others than showing up for ourselves. You may even be totally clueless about what your needs might be. Thankfully, meeting your needs is relatively simple. Not always easy, but simple. To meet your own needs, you do the following steps:

- Notice something's up
- Explore with curiosity
- Name the need
- Meet the need

It sounds simple, but it's not easy. Especially for those of us who fight against even knowing we have a need, let alone figuring out how to meet it. This process is similar to how we explore our feelings. And, just like feelings, the more you can listen to yourself and follow through with meeting your own needs, the sooner you will be able to move beyond that need. There are many ways that clutter is actually helping to meet our needs. The sooner we can see this, and address our needs from a non-clutter perspective, the sooner we can release the clutter from our lives for good.

USING CLUTTER TO MEET YOUR NEEDS

The biggest takeaway I want you to get from this ENTIRE BOOK is that recurring clutter is helping you get your needs met. Maybe, like Val, it's helping you set boundaries with your family. Or like Sienna, it's comforting you through a challenging life situation. Or like Gerald, it's helping you give yourself time and space for yourself. Or, like my sister and I when we were kids, it's giving you a feeling of security and safety. However, clutter is helping you, I just want to say: way to go. I'm proud of you for finding a way to meet your needs. There's nothing wrong with you. You've done a great job solving something that felt unmanageable. Now, let's get those needs met without the clutter. In a more direct, effective, and lasting way.

There are two simple steps that will help you effectively meet your needs, without using recurring clutter:

Step 1 – Identify what need the clutter is meeting for you, and how it's helping you.

Step 2 – Get that need met in a healthy, non-clutter way.

This sounds so simple, but it's hands down the most important thing I can offer you on your clutter-clearing journey. It's the missing piece that has been keeping you stuck in the chaos.

Use your clutter to discover what needs are being met, and then find a non-clutter solution to get that need met.

ABOUT TRAUMA AND NEEDS

Not being able to recognize your own needs might be a trauma response. A trauma response is a set of responses that one might develop when confronted with a threatening or abusive situation. Over time this becomes a habit that we retain, even when the threat or trauma is not present. These responses can keep our nervous system dysregulated and "stuck" in the trauma.

Sometimes when we were kids, it wasn't safe to have preferences or needs. And we learned that it was safer for us to abandon our own needs. If that is the case, know that you don't have to continue living that way. You can choose to put that coping mechanism down and start to invite your own needs and preferences to the party. This is easier said than done, so you might need the support of a trauma-informed therapist or other healing modality. That support may bridge a necessary gap for you to be able to step fully into your life, without the need for clutter and chaos to support you.

RESISTANCE TO SEEING CLUTTER WISDOM

Sometimes these clutter insights are like a balm to one's soul. But for others it's really hard to hear or even begin to imagine this is true.

I had a client, Raquel, who wanted to get a handle on her clutter. As we explored the timeline of her clutter, it surfaced that her clutter began when she moved into her house and shortly after she lost her baby during childbirth. The unpacked boxes still sat untouched in her house, over two decades after she lost her baby. She didn't have a clutter issue; she had a trauma that needed to be acknowledged, healed, and addressed. She stepped away from organizing and into the office of a trusted therapist. As she heals the trauma, the clutter will not be needed to hide the pain that has been buried there since she moved in. She needed a buffer to help her weather the pain of that loss. As she got stronger and healed more, she was ready to face the truth buried in her clutter.

Things aren't always simple to solve. Sometimes, in the inability to solve something, we discover a deeper issue that needs to be resolved or met, in order to solve the thing that we're focused on. This isn't you avoiding the problem or allowing yourself to become distracted. This is you allowing the clutter to bring you to the healing that is waiting for you in your body, mind, and soul.

If this is the case in your life, please be patient with

yourself. The path to healing is a long and deep one – and you are worth every step. Thank the clutter for bringing this to your attention and shift your attention to the real issue that needs and wants to be healed. And it's okay if you're not quite ready yet. This is your journey, and it will happen on your timeline. You get to choose. Remember, your intuition will keep lovingly calling you home toward the path that is meant for you. Sometimes, we just aren't ready yet, and that's okay.

The clutter has been hiding a deeper need for quite a while. And you may have not been ready to face this truth yet. You still might not be ready. That's okay. This is an open invitation. You have unlimited chances to learn this. If it's not the right time for you at this moment, I have full faith the right time will align for you. All I want you to do is to be open to the possibility that something deeper is happening in your clutter. That's all. Just imagine a world where your clutter is a kind friend who is trying to help you thrive by showing you important patterns in your life.

What I know to be true is that sometimes it can be scary to hold this insight. And the best thing we can do is to move on faith until you see the truth buried in your clutter. Name that you feel resistance but are open to a solution. Speak your truth. When you speak and honor your truth (even about resistance), you set yourself free. When the cause of your recurring clutter seems rooted in superficial solutions (organizing know-how, lack of time, etc.), lean in a little deeper. Ask yourself, "if the clutter was pointing to something deeper, what might it be?" Be open to seeing something deeper hidden in your clutter. You'll be amazed at what's waiting there for you.

The goal is not for you to become some sort of clutter wizard, but to make peace with yourself through your clutter. To hear the truth that is being spoken through your stuff, and to turn that insight into action. To stop needing the clutter to speak and act on your behalf.

Listen to your intuition. It's like the layers of an onion. You will get a different answer today than you did yesterday or you will tomorrow. Trust you will be guided to what needs attention today. You don't have to do it all. Allow the stuff to move and evolve you. It will awaken you deeply when (and if) it's right for you.

TURN INSIGHT INTO ACTION

I know at first sight the concept of clutter meeting your needs can feel a bit confusing. So, let's transform this insight into a practical action that you can easily apply to your life and stuff. Look around your house and choose a pattern of recurring clutter, something that never stays organized no matter how hard you try. It might be shoes, unopened mail, your entryway clutter, items by your nightstand, or the entire garage. Go and look at this space. Allow yourself to really be present with the clutter. Without judging it (or yourself). Ask yourself how the clutter might be helping you? Is it keeping people out? Is it allowing you to avoid the pain of looking at bills you don't have the money to pay? Is it helping you ask your partner for something? What is it doing for you? How is it helping?

Once you have an idea of how the clutter is helping you, I want you to start to explore non-clutter solutions for that need. Write out at least ten non-clutter ways you can get that need met. Allow yourself to get really creative in coming up with alternative ways to meet that need.

Once you've had time to brainstorm, I want you to pick one option you want to try and apply to your life right now. For example, Gerald might use this insight of knowing he needs time alone on his drives to set a boundary with others by saying, "my time alone in the car is my sacred time, and I don't do carpooling." Or maybe he'll switch to a Vespa. Or buy super pretty but uncomfortable seat covers (that deter people from riding with him). Or rip his front passenger seat out entirely. I joke, but the sky is the limit. Get creative when it comes to meeting your needs. There's always a solution out there for you.

There are infinite ways to meet your needs more directly, without the clutter. The more practical you can make the solutions the better. Clutter has this nebulous feeling that keeps us from feeling clear, grounded, and strong. So, the more practical the solutions the better. If Sienna had chosen a solution like "take more time alone for myself," that may not have worked. The practical solution of getting a dog, allowed her to truly create an unshakeable sense of comfort and love in her home. We're often so quick to dismiss our own needs. But giving ourselves something concrete can be a game changer.

Once you choose the option you want to try first, apply it to your life now. If that doesn't work, you have nine other possibilities to try. We're looking for non-clutter solutions for meeting your needs. When you start taking action toward meeting your needs without the clutter, that's when you can experience true freedom. This takes practice but when you start to reclaim your power and turn your clutter wisdom into action, that's when clutter will fall away and not return. That is how clutter can change your life and transform you in brilliant ways.

10

STOP STRUGGLING WITH CLUTTER ONCE AND FOR ALL

I need to ask you a challenging question. It may be a little difficult to consider, but please bear with me. What if things never change? What if you never get organized and things stay exactly how they are – or get worse. What would that be like for you? Would you feel okay and be able to keep on living your life? Or do you feel like the clutter would suck your life force, be a drain on you and your loved ones, or cost you the joy in your life? Making changes that you are ready to make requires doing things radically differently. And at a much different pace than you're used to. But it's totally worth it. You're here right now because you know it's time for a change. You're ready. Something inside of you feels like you're late for your own life. That you should have been organized ten years ago. So, you keep speeding through, starting projects, getting overwhelmed, and then walking away from projects mid-way through and either starting new projects (that you also don't finish) or turning on the TV and checking out. It's time for something different. The voice that tells you you're late, behind, or totally incapable of doing this is not helping you, it's sabotaging you. Don't give it the power. Take your power back and know that there's a way to experience clarity, peace of mind, and organization that you've never even thought of before. A way through that leads you to be impenetrable to clutter and chaos. A way through that finds you standing in your power and joy, with clutter unable to touch your fierce presence in your life.

You've been down this road before. You know the one. Where you learn new organizing skills, get excited, and then get lost in the chaos – again. What will it take for this time to be your last time? What will it take to make sure that this isn't another failed organizing attempt? I know it may seem impossible, especially because you've never experienced true relief from clutter before, but I promise you, this is 100 percent possible. But for you to truly put the clutter behind you, there are a few things you need to understand.

YOU'RE NEVER DONE

Let's just get the most annoying truth out of the way. There is no world where clutter is gone forever. As long as we're in the physical world, we're always going to have to deal with stuff. This world was born of chaos and matter. Even if you're a stark minimalist, you will always have to engage with and make decisions about physical objects in this world, and sometimes this means rightfully refusing them access to your life. The non-sexy truth is that you're never done with clutter because "stuff" is a part of this modern world. And as long as you have stuff, there will always be a need to organize, purge, and refuse objects that cross your path. It's just a part of life.

Let this be an insight that doesn't defeat you but adds to the clear intention of surrounding yourself only with things you truly love and want. Stop keeping that cheetah print candle your Aunt Joan gave you, but that you secretly hate. Release those skinny jeans that you haven't worn in 10 years. Choose to include things in your life and home that bring you joy, remind you of who you are today, and that will help you evolve into the person you're becoming.

Organizing is a journey, not a task. If you can stop trying to "get it all done yesterday," you'll stop feeling behind. And you'll be able to see the insight that your clutter has in store for you. As long as you're in a material world, there will be stuff to deal with. Yes, you can get to a point where the stuff doesn't weigh on you as much, and where it's easier to manage and tolerate. That's the whole point of this book. But know that this shift in perspective takes time. This is a journey. It takes daily practice, but soon you'll stop feeling tortured by your stuff. You'll know what to do and how to do it best for you, your brain, and your life. Knowing that the act of organizing is a journey, not a destination will help you face the road ahead.

HOPE IS A BLINDFOLD

It's easy to believe that if only you were organized, life would be easier, better, or perfect. Organizing can make life easier, absolutely. But, in a world of chaos, it's time to remove the blindfold of hope that having an organized home will be some sort of savior. Unless you identify the truth in your clutter, the chaos will only return. We have to stop seeing clutter as the enemy, and start to see the process of organizing as a healing one. Just as clutter holds insights about you, organizing will reveal the true you. It will help give you a safe space to come home to yourself, but it isn't a magical potion that will end all the pain and suffering in your life. What it will do is transform organizing into a lifeline for understanding yourself and setting yourself free. It will give you a method to experience control in an out-of-control world. And it is a skill set that will help you evolve your life and spaces to better support you anytime you need that.

Remember as a kid how exciting it was to rearrange your bedroom furniture or build a fort in the living room? Organizing can give you that joyful feeling again. It can be a playground for you to explore, play, and shift the energy and perspective of your home and life. You'll go from feeling like you're buried in an avalanche, to feeling inspired and capable of changing your home (and world) to better support you. Organizing is power. And clutter is the source that awakens that power for you.

TIMES OF BIG CHANGE

Even if you get perfectly organized today, things happen in our lives that are out of our control. Your aunt might pass away, and you inherit her possessions. Or your parents decide to gift you every keepsake and piece of school artwork you ever created as they lighten the load in their attic. Or you may decide to downsize and need to get rid of things that won't fit in your new space. There will be times in life when clutter will come back into your life again. The beauty is that everything you've learned here will help you stop the chaos before it roots into your life.

Physical objects don't have to be clutter. They become clutter when we don't know what to do about them. You now have a whole toolbox of skills for how to deal with the stuff in your life; before it turns into clutter that sticks to every surface of your life. The skills you've learned in this book about organizing, facing big feelings, and the wisdom buried in your clutter will help you handle those situations in such drastically different ways. They won't derail your life, home, clarity, and peace of mind.

You now have the power and skills to manage the stuff that comes into your life. You know how to not let stuff become permanently rooted. Knowing you have the skills to manage anything that comes into your life is way more powerful than you never getting a scrap of clutter again. This wisdom makes you impervious to the chaos of the world because you now know how to face and handle it. It makes you resilient in infinite ways.

THE POWER OF COMPLETION

Clutter is a magnet for more clutter. One of the most powerful things you can do to make sure clutter stays gone for good is to complete your organizing projects. I had a client, Sam, who had me help her organize her entire home. In the end, there was one box of paperwork she didn't think was important enough to deal with. She was burned out from organizing paper and didn't think that it would matter much if we just put it in the garage and forgot about it. Two years later, I was back because Sam's house had backslid into chaos again. As we completed round two of her whole home organizing, we came across that same box of paperwork. Once again, Sam didn't want to finish it, saying it wasn't that important. This time, I insisted, and we organized the box together. It took less than thirty minutes and was much easier than she thought. After we finished that box of paperwork, her paper clutter never returned. And her home stayed organized.

There is something about the power of completion that allows organization to become a lasting state. When you come across that last box, bag, or drawer, take the time to complete it. It's normal to feel agitated, angry, or overwhelmed when you hit that last box. Feel those feelings and do it anyway. When you are able to see your project through to the end, it takes the magnetic pull away from your clutter. It's like blocking all clutter from returning. Our brain sees clutter and thinks, "Oh good, that's where the clutter goes." But if it sees a beautiful, clean space, that same clutter feels like a violation, and we hit an internal road bump that invites us to recalibrate and find a home for that clutter instead of allowing it to build up.

THE PERFECT IMPERFECTION OF LIVING WITH OTHERS

Ah, other people! Life would be so easy if we only had to deal with our own stuff, right? That can definitely be true sometimes, but there is such richness in what relationships with other people bring into our lives. But when you share spaces with people, it can definitely create challenges. If you live with other people, it's vital to make peace with imperfection.

Everyone's brains work so uniquely. How you think may not at all be how other people think. It's important to allow them the dignity of their own journey. Their version of "clean" may not look like yours, and that's okay.

Find layers of acceptance and peace with yourself and focus on your own projects, possessions, and spaces. This will stop a lot of frustration and chaos. Get clarity around what you need and release the things that are out of your control.

When I lived with my ex-fiancé and his three kids, I had to adjust quickly to the fact that I couldn't have a perfectly minimalist house, the way I do when I live on my own. There were always piles of homework, clean laundry to fold, and overflowing toys out in the garage. When I tried to make them adjust to my expectations, things felt stressful for everyone. When I started to lean in and find solutions that worked for all of us (and stopped caring so much about what other people would think when they came into the home of "Star Hansen, Professional Organizer") we all felt more at ease and peaceful.

ARE YOU THE GATEKEEPER?

If you are the primary person organizing and caring for the home, it's easy to become the gatekeeper of the organizing projects. Now, this might be okay with you if you want things done a certain way. But it's also possible that you don't want to manage the organizing alone and doing so may fill you with resentment and anger.

Being the primary keeper of the organizing (and other home tasks) can be quite lonely, and it's important for you to know what you need and to ask for help. You're not Atlas, and it's not your job to carry the whole world. There will be things you have to release control of and allow them to be perfectly imperfect. You will need to ask for help sometimes. You will also have to set firm boundaries about what's not okay or healthy for you. This is a journey, and the clutter will, once again, help you to take care of yourself in beautiful ways.

Make sure to include the people you share spaces with in the creation phase of the organizing systems so they're built to work for everyone in the house. This will allow other people to have input as to how the systems are set up and take some of that pressure off of you. This may include family, roommates, and even those who work in your home such as babysitters, housekeepers, etc. Make sure to communicate expectations and get their agreement regarding if they're willing to do their part. And for kids, make sure the expectations and consequences are clear and fair.

STOP FACING CLUTTER ALONE

Speaking of dealing with clutter on your own. I highly recommend you not. Organizing can be a great therapeutic solo activity, much like how some people wash dishes to feel a sense of control over their lives. But if you have any layers of shame, overwhelm, or insecurity around your clutter, I highly recommend you reach out and get support. Remember, sharing is the antidote to shame. The voices in your head will tell you that your clutter is horribly embarrassing and that it's worse than everyone else. They will tell you that people will shame you and you should keep it to yourself. As the old saying goes, we're only as sick as our secrets. As long as you keep your clutter hidden away out of sight, the more that shame grows and feels true. Community is one of the best ways to fast-track your organizing journey. It's vital for you to find a safe community to walk this path with. Take the time to find people who feel safe and healthy for you.

Wondering where you can find these magical unicorns? They're everywhere, it just takes a little looking. Support can look like a safe community, like the Chaos to Calm Organizing Community(www.starhansen.com/community), working with a professional organizer (NAPO, NABPO, ICD are great places to find skilled, safe experts near you), or even buddying up with a friend.

All that matters is that you start to make progress in a safe, fun community that allows you to love yourself more deeply, be more productive, and have a good time (and yes, it is possible to have fun while organizing). Organizing in community is a great way to heal deeply together and to realize you're not alone. This is truly the key to lasting change in behavior and mindset. And the "I'm not alone in this" effect is powerful. When you share something vulnerable and someone else nods their head yes or identifies with what you've shared, you start to realize even more deeply that there's nothing wrong with you and you are loveable exactly as you are, clutter and all!

As an organizer, I see the healing power of being present to people's clutter every day. People's clutter – the "horrible shameful secret" that they thought would send me running for the hills screaming, becomes a healing balm, as they noticed that I didn't fire them and leave the house terrified of their chaos.

During the pandemic, I realized that people needed a safe space to work together as they were isolated in their homes. I created a virtual group organizing session called the Organizing Playground. On a regular basis, a group of us fired up our computers and organized together online. The first time we did it, I thought we would be there for two hours; seven hours later, we had made so much progress we could hardly believe it, and it was actually fun. Since then, we do regular Playground Sessions in the Chaos to Calm Community. It can truly be a lifesaver and a great way to make progress when you feel stuck or overwhelmed.

The reasons why this type of support is so effective is the same reason why it's helpful to have a friend or organizer with you while decluttering. There's a concept called Body Doubling, wherein just by having someone with you, you hold yourself more accountable, are more focused, more productive, and have more fun. Plus, it normalizes the challenges that so many people have around their clutter, and it greatly reduces shame and overwhelm. If I was going to offer one lifeline to getting and staying organized, it would be to find a safe, supportive community to organize with. There's truly no downside to organizing with a safe, loving community, especially once you realize that they're just like you and won't go running for the hills when they see your kitchen countertop.

STEER CLEAR OF UNSAFE PEOPLE

Now, to be clear, there are tons of people who are actually very unsafe to work on your clutter with. Let's steer clear of them. You know the ones, the people who judge you, want to tell you how you're doing things wrong, gloat about their lack of issues with clutter, or who tell your secrets to others. I've seen partners, friends, and family make jabs and say horrible things, such as "Let's see if you can keep this up," even after someone got organized and had maintained it for a significant amount of time.

You don't need that kind of negative energy in your life. Let's just name that those people are unsafe and do not deserve your vulnerability or to share in your journey with clutter. There are plenty of other people to walk this path with. You don't need to include anyone unsafe in your clutter healing journey.

Take time to look for people who are safe to include on your clutter journey. People who are compassionate, supportive, and who keep your secrets. People who see the best in you and remind you of that truth, even when you forget. These are the people who are safe to walk this path with.

As you make progress on your organizing journey, make sure that you don't circle back to unsafe people to try to get their validation. You don't need their approval to know that you're doing a good job. The only person whose opinion matters is your own. Other people's opinions often say way more about where they are in their lives than about how you're doing. Remember, this is a practice. Lean into the practice of noticing if something works for you, and how YOU feel about what you've done.

Disinvite negative, unhealthy people from your organizing journey (let's get wild, how about disinviting them from your whole life). Stick with positive people who cheer you on, support you unconditionally and validate the great work you're doing.

JUST SAY NO

One of the skills that organizing will teach you, and require of you, is boundaries. At its simplest, organizing is all about creating and maintaining boundaries. As you get organized, you refine this skill. This is a continual practice. Every time someone gives you a grab bag at a party that you know will just end up abandoned on your closet floor or a two-for-one deal at the store on makeup you really only need one of, those are opportunities to strengthen your boundaries. It can be a hard lesson to learn and sometimes feel counterintuitive, but no is a complete sentence.

A big part of organizing is saying no to bringing unwanted things into your house. You are not obligated to anyone (and I mean *anyone*) to bring stuff you don't want into your home. If you have a rowboat that's sinking because it has a hole in it, you've got to plug the hole where the water is coming in, not just dump the water back out of the boat. Patching the hole is the same as saying no to unwanted things in your home and life.

BE INTENTIONAL

Filling our homes with only the things we truly want requires us to make conscious decisions. That can look like you making time to find what you really want. Or spending a little bit more money to get the *right* thing that you actually want, instead of something that doesn't really meet your needs.

We've all kept those jeans that weren't quite right because we couldn't find what we really wanted. Or maybe we found what we wanted but couldn't or didn't want to spend the money for the designer jeans that fit us just right. Or maybe we held onto things we didn't like because we didn't have the bandwidth to figure out what we truly needed or wanted.

Take the time to find the right thing for you and say no to everything else. Sometimes the first step to decluttering is shopping and finding the thing you actually need, so you can say no to what doesn't work for you.

CAN YOU BORROW IT INSTEAD?

There are so many things that we have in our home and only use once in a while. Is it possible for you to borrow something instead of owning it? The idea of communal possessions is one of my favorite concepts. Imagine people pooling together to share resources? For many years, that's how people in communities lived. We can awaken that way of thinking today.

Don't feel like you need to purchase everything you will ever use. Some items, like tools, can be rented from hardware stores. And, sometimes, you can borrow things from friends or neighbors. There are many options available to make sure you're not constantly acquiring things you truly don't want or need. It's a practice, but one worth investing time in developing.

DIVINE TIMING

One thing that often causes people to backslide into chaos again is timing. We have this skewed perspective that we're behind or will never get done. We get overwhelmed, throw our hands up and walk away; another failed attempt behind us. But what if you're actually perfectly on time – even when you get distracted or sidelined? I can't tell you how many times I've been working with someone on their office or bedroom, when suddenly a pipe bursts in the bathroom and we have to change directions and organize the now flooded room.

Trust that something bigger than yourself is guiding you along the way. Also, your home has great wisdom and knows where your energy is most needed. Sometimes, we can make the most progress when we're "doing" nothing but thinking, planning, or resting. When I'm organizing a room in my own home, I often spend a lot of time just looking at the space and daydreaming before I begin. There's something powerful about the ability to feel the space, and mentally explore it without achieving some big goal. That practice makes things go so much better for me. Usually when I feel the pull for me to take action on my organizing project, the project is completed so quickly because I'm aligned with the space and my divine timing.

Trust your divine timing. Be gentle on yourself. Sometimes we just need more time. This is not the time for your inner critic to step forward. This is when we want to get softer and gentler with ourselves. Big changes that are being invited through your clutter can feel terrifying and you may not be ready yet. That's okay. You can learn the truth without changing your whole life. You're the boss, you determine your path and timeline.

What if you're not late? What if you're right on time? You're right where you're supposed to be. You're never late or in trouble. You're on your own perfect path. And there's no such thing as failure here.

GIVE YOURSELF A GOAL

I tell clients that if they want to get organized quickly, plan a party. This will kick you into gear every time. I worked with this amazing woman whose big organizing breakthroughs happened when she started planning parties. The parties would give her a deadline for her projects and encouraged her to maintain her progress. That's not a crutch, it's a smart and powerful tool.

Now, you don't have to throw a party in order to get organized. But having a goal or a deadline for yourself will do wonders for getting (and staying) organized. The idea of being organized for the sake of being organized isn't very inspiring. We all want to be organized in order to experience something else in our lives more fully. Create a deadline or goal that weaves that desire into your life. And make it practical and tangible. Giving yourself some sort of tangible goal at the end of your organizing project will help inspire action, motivate you to keep going, and give you an element of accountability.

TURNING INSIGHT INTO ACTION

Make a list of what makes you happy and joyful. How can you start to integrate those into your life right now, even in one small way. Do one thing from the list a day. Want to dance but can never find time or money for a class? Turn on the radio and jam out to your favorite song. Want to have a party but feel too overwhelmed to have people over to your house? Have a picnic outside.

Things don't have to be perfect. You can start right now, exactly where you are. You deserve it! Live your life fully without waiting for clutter to go away; it's a surefire recipe to evict the clutter. It's common to want to wait until we're done completely with organizing before we feel like we have "earned" living our life to the fullest. Think about all the things you are waiting to do until you're totally organized. How many of those can you do right now, clutter and all? I bet most of them.

Stop waiting until you're totally organized to live your life. You've got to live your life fully now – without waiting for your clutter to go away. Fill your space with life, not stuff. The more you experience your life, the less space there will be for clutter. I promise, it will find its way out of your life and home. Don't waste another moment waiting for your life to start. Live now. Start now. Don't waste your joy, live it now – imperfections, clutter, and all. This is your life, and you only get this time around to play.

11

THE PATH AHEAD

You've done it! You've seen the truth buried in your clutter. You've been brave, strong, and self-loving. You chose to be willing to see your clutter in a different light, and you've now given yourself the tools to never be a victim of clutter again.

You learned the organizing skills you needed to have in order to not let the process of organizing trip you up. These skills will continue to grow the more you practice them, and they are something that cannot be taken away from you. Now that you know this, you've taken the power away from the clutter and put it back into your own hands.

You got to know why your inner critic makes organizing feel like torture. And how intuition is the antidote for your inner critic. Plus, you've seen how organizing can help you develop trust and confidence in yourself.

You've learned how to handle the number one thing that derails your organizing process – uncomfortable feelings. You learned that uncomfortable feelings are a part of organizing, not a failure or a breakdown in the organizing process. You've learned how to handle those feelings and some key strategies to see you through the moments when they arise while you're organizing.

You've discovered how the rooms of your home show you the areas of your life that are blocked or are out of whack. Armed with this information, you can see how clutter is directing you to an area of life that needs attention, and once you have shifted your focus, the clutter won't be necessary.

You've also tapped into your clutter wisdom by realizing that clutter isn't random. And that within your clutter, you have endless insights available to you. Your clutter exposes patterns in your life and starts to show you how to free yourself from them.

And most importantly, you've learned the ways that clutter is helping you get your needs met. This is one of the most important insights because once you understand how clutter is helping you, you can get those needs met in healthy, non-clutter-based ways. And once your clutter no longer has to meet your needs, you're able to release the clutter with ease (and way faster than you would expect).

Plus, you've learned some key insights for how to make sure clutter stays gone once you've released it and some powerful keys to make the process of organizing more effective and less painful. Organizing can actually be fun and healing, and now you know how to make it feel that way for yourself.

This book is an invitation for you to see your clutter, yourself, and your life differently. You can stop working through friction and chaos and start to move with ease and collaboration through your life seeing how the clutter is actually a friend and confidant who is helping you to come home to yourself. This is a powerful journey. And it's one that will save your life. Knowing that you no longer need to struggle will set you free.

As you eliminate your chaos, you can start to live your genius. Everything you need is already within you. One of the interesting things that happens when I organize a space with someone is that often there is an organizing "solution" found within the chaos. Meaning, they already have bins, bags, or old empty shoe boxes in their clutter, something we can use as a container or a solution, without them having to buy anything new. They can buy something new, but the truth is that their basic needs are almost always met by using what they already had. The same is true internally. It often feels like we are broken, and our clutter is proof of that. But the truth is that you have everything you will ever need within you. Every bit of strength, genius and power is already within you right now. All you need to do is remember this and then start living from that knowing. You deserve to be that beautiful, blazing, powerful version of you. You make this world better just by being you.

There are countless people who have turned their clutter into a life they love, going from feeling like their home is some sort of punishment to feeling like they are living out loud with joy and freedom. That is what you have now. The skills to be your own success story.

Bobbi's dining room clutter made her think she was going crazy. It covered every surface and made it feel like she could never relax in her home, let alone have people over. The last few decades had not been what she expected or wanted from her life. She did her best to create happiness within the chaos, but she found herself drowning in stuff and feeling uncertain about the life she created. She was on the verge of leaving her partner, felt invisible in her life, and felt overwhelmed every time she came home. She hired me secretly hoping that if she was organized, she would be able to start over again and finally be happy. While organizing, we discovered an organic apple hidden in the clutter under her table. She had hidden it there in an attempt at keeping something for herself. In a home and family where nothing felt sacred or meant for her alone, she needed to know that she deserved something good. The beautiful apple she had hidden to enjoy on her own, without the worry of her partner or kids eating it while she was at work, was now rotten and molding in a reusable tote. She felt like that apple. As though she had to tuck the best parts of her away until it was safe to come back out again but feeling like she was dying inside. Seeing this apple made her realize the ways she was not getting her needs met. That apple awakened a part of her that would no longer hold back her voice. It propelled her forward into a journey of learning how to communicate, claim self-confidence, and create boundaries for herself. She stopped holding back her needs and started to advocate for herself. She reclaimed the spaces of her home, released responsibility for taking care of others who were equipped to take care of themselves, and set herself free. She stopped waiting for the clutter to go away before she enjoyed her life. She traveled, started hosting holidays at her house again, and bought the car of her dreams. She started to organize thinking that she would leave her life, and instead organizing gave her the skills to enjoy the life she had.

Things often get messier before they tidy up, and this is a part of the process. But now you're armed with the skills needed to see yourself through these challenges. And I know you can do this.

My wish for you as you move forward in your life with this powerful new insight is that you remember that you're never alone. That there is a whole community of people walking the same path and you don't have to be alone in this ever again. I want you to know that you're capable of doing hard things. And that you have the skills to see you through. Even when things are challenging, I want you to know that they won't stay that way. Change is the most constant thing in life. I want you to know that your clutter is a friend, and it has massive insight that will help you heal and transform and change your life in all the ways you've been craving. I want you to hear your own truth more than you hear any negative voices outside of yourself. For you to not need outside proof to know you're enough. To be so strong in your love for yourself that when you see the chaos of the world, your heart breaks open to greater love. For compassion to take the place of judgment and for curiosity to be your new fuel.

You deserve a life of joy. One where you are the hero, not the villain. Your clutter is also not the villain. It's more of a guide, here to help illuminate the way. A beacon of truth that will point the way home. And it offers you endless wisdom. And now you're ready to hear it.

Reach for this book when you get lost. When it feels like you're not sure how to make things feel less chaotic in your world, I hope these pages illuminate wisdom that will see you home. That's all I want for you. I want *you* to be the safe harbor you crave in this life. And for you to stop seeing clutter and chaos as the enemy but instead, as the map home. Understanding your clutter is like having a deep conversation with yourself. Some truths are hard to see, but next to those challenging truths are gems that shine beautiful light into your world. And they're worth digging for.

Amidst the chaos in life, something precious is buried there too. The you that you've been becoming. The insight and wisdom that you have learned with each step. And the more you hear and believe in that wisdom, the less you will need the chaos and painful lessons. Look at each speck of clutter as either a confirmation of your magic or a wonderful guide steering you forward.

You're ready to take on the clutter of your life. But I don't expect you to do it all at once. I want you to follow your wisdom. Pick the path that feels the most open and empowering to you. Look for the starting point that is most welcoming to you. Something that feels full of excitement, possibility, or hope. Don't punish yourself by doing the hardest thing first. Go slowly, take deep breaths, and move a step at a time. You'll get there. With each step your power grows and soon you won't need clutter anymore.

The days of your clutter holding you back are done. It's time. Your time. Everything has led you here and you're ready. You've got this. And I've got you. Onward, my wonderful friend!

ACKNOWLEDGMENTS

I would like to thank Dr. Angela Lauria, Natasa Smirnov, Madeline Kosten, and the whole team at Difference Press for sharing their genius and helping me bring my vision to life.

For all my clients – especially those who became friends. You knock my socks off. You make work never actually feel like work. Thank you for allowing me to go on this journey with you. Thank you for trusting me with your hearts and homes and welcoming me in like family. Thank you for your bravery, vulnerability, and perseverance. I'm so honored to know you and love you exactly as you are – clutter and all!

I would like to thank the amazing Tracy Cook, for being the incredible person you are. Thanks for letting me write this book for you. And thanks for serving as quality control, cheerleader, and sage. This book wouldn't have happened without you. I'm so grateful for the ways it brought you more deeply into my life and enhanced our friendship. And thanks to Brian and Tony for sharing you with me and tolerating our endless calls and non-stop laughter.

Thanks to Jane Deuber, for holding the light for me and helping me to stretch beyond my comfort zone. Mary Reed, thank you for taking a chance on me and being willing to go deep down the clutter rabbit hole with me. To Kathleen McCully-Parrish, Katie Lamb, and Lynda Chaikin – thank you for supporting me over the last year and beyond. Your healing magic rocks my world. Thank you for helping me turn adversity into freedom and joy.

To NAPO, NABPO, ICD, and all the organizers out there doing this sacred work. I'm so honored to be of service alongside you. Thank you for helping me navigate this road. May we all continue to grow and evolve together as we share the vision of clarity, peace, and love.

To Adam Hendershott for being the best photographer in the world and Sylvia Hendershott for styling the heck out of me. I'm still in awe that we got so many pics while Ava was down for her nap. You two are the best "family" a girl could ask for and I'm just so proud of all we've created together. It seems like only yesterday we were up at 3 a.m. brainstorming the life we're now living. I love you all so much. Family forever!

And to my besties: Carrie, thank you for your unwavering love, sisterhood, and soul connection. Being in the bubble with you is my favorite. Thank you (and Shasta) for helping me create the cover of this book. And for reminding me who I am and holding me accountable to my best self. I'm so grateful to you for paving the way, I couldn't have done this book without your support, creativity, and inspiration. Dee, John, Miles, and Leo, thank you for your unconditional love, fierce support and for making me laugh any time of the day or night. You gave me a safe place to awaken this book in my life and soul. You are the safe place I always carry with me. I love you with all my ~~fart~~ heart. Sarah, you're truly a lighthouse in a world of chaos. I love and appreciate you. You'll never know how much our first apartment together shaped the path I'm walking today. Jill, thank you for seeing what I am capable of and pushing me to be my best. Jessica, Kelsey, Lindsey, Kara, Jill, Tiffany, Donna, Elizabeth, Christy, Ryan, and so many others I haven't named but will never forget (yes, I'm talking to you). I love you and appreciate you more than words could ever say.

Huge love and gratitude to Mom, Dad, and my brother Toby. Mom, thanks for our long walks and deep conversations about life. Quality time with you has been such a special gift these past few years. You're always the first in line to support any crazy thing I dream up, and I couldn't be more grateful. Your endless support keeps me going. Dad, your teacher's soul led the way for me to walk this path. It was so fun to be writing our books at the same time. Thanks for your loving heart and endless support. Toby, thanks for being my big brother and for your excessive use of the word fuck. This title is for you. And to my huge, beautiful, rowdy family – my grandma, aunts, uncles, cousins, second cousins, cousins once removed, godchildren, (almost) step-kids, and friends that are like family. You know who you are. I'm grateful to call you all my community.

To my sister, Jena. Even though you've crossed over, you're with me every step I take. Thank you for your constant presence in my life, and for awakening something in me I never knew was possible. I carry you with me everywhere I go and will always do my best to help people come home to themselves, and discover the love hidden in their chaos.

Thank you to clutter – for being such an incredible steward of transformation. And to Creator for being so wise to hide love, freedom, and transformation in even the most chaotic of spaces.

ABOUT THE AUTHOR

Star Hansen is a Clutter Whisperer and Certified Professional Organizer©. She helps successful, badass women who feel like a hot mess to figure out why their clutter isn't going away so they can finally clear the chaos, and live a life of freedom, joy, and peace. She's the organizer you call when nothing else works!

Star has been helping people clear their clutter since 2004. Star is a member of NAPO (The National Association of Productivity & Organizing Professionals). Her organizing firm, Reveal by Star, LLC offers online courses and coaching to help people set themselves free from their clutter.

Star created the Chaos to Calm Organizing Community in 2019 to support people from across the globe in their organizing transformations. This online community has provided a safe, healing space for people to unpack what's hiding in their clutter and finally see progress after years of attempts.

Star's multi-layered approach is that of mind, body, spirit, and space. She has a knack for seeing through the chaos and into the lives and hearts of the people she works with. Her approach has been featured on OWN, TLC, HGTV, Style, A&E, and the Tyra Banks Show. She has been a contributor to *O Magazine*, *Woman's Day*, and Oprah.com. Star's humorous and thought-provoking TEDx Tucson talk explores what the monsters in your closet are trying to tell you.

Star lives in Tucson, AZ. She is an eighth generation Tucsonan who loves living in the southwest, and never misses an opportunity to soak up a desert sunrise, sunset, or monsoon downpour.

Website: www.starhansen.com
Email: hello@starhansen.com
Facebook: www.facebook.com/starhansen
Instagram: www.instagram.com/star.hansen
Pinterest: www.pinterest.com/starhansen

OTHER OFFERINGS BY STAR HANSEN

www.starhansen.com/courses

Chaos to Calm Organizing Community

www.starhansen.com/community

The Meaning of Stuff

www.starhansen.com/meaningofstuff

10 Steps to (Finally!) Get and Stay Organized

www.starhansen.com/10steps

Overcoming Overwhelm

https://starhansen.com/overcomingoverwhelm

Decluttering Love

https://starhansen.com/declutteringlove

Time Management Transformation

https://starhansen.com/workfromhome/

Work from Home

https://starhansen.com/workfromhome/

ABOUT DIFFERENCE PRESS

Difference Press is the publishing arm of The Author Incubator, an Inc. 500 award-winning company that helps business owners and executives grow their brand, establish thought leadership, and get customers, clients, and highly-paid speaking opportunities, through writing and publishing books.

While traditional publishers require that you already have a large following to guarantee they make money from sales to your existing list, our approach is focused on using a book to grow your following – even if you currently don't have a following. This is why we charge an up-front fee but never take a percentage of revenue you earn from your book.

☞ MORE THAN A COACH. MORE THAN A PUBLISHER. ✍

We work intimately and personally with each of our authors to develop a revenue-generating strategy for the book. By using a Lean Startup style methodology, we guarantee the book's success before we even start writing. We provide all the technical support authors need with editing, design, marketing, and publishing, the emotional support you would get from a book coach to help you manage anxiety and time constraints, and we serve as a strategic thought partner engineering the book for success.

The Author Incubator has helped almost 2,000 entrepreneurs write, publish, and promote their non-fiction books. Our authors have used their books to gain international media exposure, build a brand and marketing following, get lucrative speaking engagements, raise awareness of their product or service, and attract clients and customers.

☞ ARE YOU READY TO WRITE A BOOK? ✍

As a client, we will work with you to make sure your book gets done right and that it gets done quickly. The Author Incubator provides one-stop for strategic book consultation, author coaching to manage writer's block and anxiety, full-service professional editing, design, and self-publishing services, and book marketing and launch campaigns. We sell this as one package so our clients are not slowed down with contradictory advice. We have a 99 percent success rate with nearly all of our clients completing their books, publishing them, and reaching bestseller status upon launch.

☞ APPLY NOW AND BE OUR NEXT SUCCESS STORY ✍

To find out if there is a significant ROI for you to write a book, get on our calendar by completing an application at www.TheAuthorIncubator.com/apply.

OTHER BOOKS BY DIFFERENCE PRESS

Profitable Salon Owner: Rise Above the Chaos In Your Business and Reignite Your Passion and Profits by Jason Everett

Leadership Recreated: A Woman's Guide to Surviving and Thriving in Patriarchal Academia by Kem Gambrell, Ph.D.

Happy Gay Christian Hereafter: 8 Steps to Reconcile Your Identity to Family and Faith or Leave without Regret by Carter Neill Holmes

Talk More, Fight Less: Rebuilding, Renewing, and Restoring Communication in Your Relationship by Dr. Sandra W. Ingram

Starting and Serving: Your Personal Guide to Launching a Successful, New Career as a Nonprofit Leader by R. Romona Jackson, Esq.

The Photographer's Path: Do What You Love, Tell Client's Stories through Images, and Have the Business of Your Dreams by Maya Manseau

Marathon in the Fog: Supporting a Parent with Dementia in Life and Death by Jennifer Olden, LMFT

THANK YOU

I'm so grateful that you opened this book and are willing to discover why your clutter hasn't gone away yet and what you can do about it.

Not sure what to do next? Good news! You don't have to know what comes next, I'm here to help you with that. My job is to guide you in turning your insight into action.

To help you, I've created a free class as a thank you for reading this book and inviting me to be a part of your journey!

Visit www.starhansen.com/bookgift for a free class helping you to take the next steps in clearing your clutter for good.

I know that together we can figure out why your clutter hasn't gone away so you can take your power back and never struggle with clutter again.

Made in the USA
Middletown, DE
15 February 2023

24867944R00104